Learning Burney

A MAP OF MY
MOTHER AND ME

ASHLEY CLEVELAND

A WARMING TREND

This book began as a story that became a conversation. The story was delivered by my mother, Burney to a large group of women at a retreat. She'd taken a class on writing and presenting pieces of her life in prose, filling numerous legal pads writing and rewriting. I glanced at one on a visit and read: "All the world's a stage…" 'Oh boy, I thought, here we go'.

In truth and in Burney's life, all the world is a stage. She dresses and accessorizes to go to the mailbox and I was glad to be on hand for her presentation because not only is she well groomed, she is interesting and shocking and very funny too. I heard her on the morning of in her little galley kitchen, enunciating, modulating, delivering. I assumed I knew the gist of her narrative, highlights and lowlights, told and retold over the years but I was unprepared for the schooling she gave me and at the end of her 30 minute talk, my first thought was: 'This is a book.'

I am a career singer, songwriter and musician but I took a detour with a memoir in 2013 and found that I loved the generosity of prose, the opportunity to expand an idea into a paragraph. I'd initially tried that with songwriting until my first publisher told me: "Ashley, no one is interested in your second page of lyrics."

Over the years I've tightened up my lyrics though I don't think I've yet achieved Paul McCartney's assertion that 25 words a song is ideal. But once I surrendered to the opportunity to fill not one blank page but a book of them, I was all in.

Taking an idea from my friend Lydia, I'd given Burney a little journal called 75 things I like about you for her 75th birthday, filling each page with anecdotes and observations. Now I thought I could start by expanding that idea into a book of essays comprising my mother's life and call it: "Eighty-Five Things I Like About You". I met with a freelance editor early on and she said, "First of all, that's a lousy book title and secondly, you've lost about half your potential readers because not all of them, including me, like their mothers." I don't know why these things didn't occur to me—I too understand the tension that exists between parents and their children. I understand it as a daughter—and as a mother too.

I have not always liked Burney. Her power and presence can read like certitude and as I was beginning to form I generally felt there was a 'but' in her assessment of me. Add the instability of alcoholism, a sham marriage to my closeted gay father, divorce and a cross-country move and my childhood starts to distill down to a single word: disaster.

One thing Burney and my father Jim shared in common was a love of presentation and performance. Both of them were beautiful, both accomplished and confident. I was the first born and a child of great promise in my parents eyes. I have a photo of them holding me as a newborn, lifted up and out like Simba as if to say: Here she is, the best of both of us, the consolation to this unhappy union, the one who will carry it all forward. But I didn't, I couldn't. I wasn't the girl they were expecting.

From childhood all the way to this third act—a euphemism for early old age (actually 'early' is slightly euphemistic and maybe overly hopeful too), I have, in many ways, remained the family outsider, keeping everyone at an emotional and geographic distance, choosing to make a life elsewhere. Some of that was career driven—but some was wound driven. And though I have worked tirelessly in therapy and recovery to resolve those wounds, there is a cold spot in me that persists.

Unsurprisingly, when I presented the idea of a book to my mother she liked it and agreed. I told her I would take her legal pads to rewrite and expand her narrative. I would also need her to be available for interviews; this seems fairly straight forward and reasonable but reaching Burney is often

2

difficult. She's a person who thrives on business and leaves her phone under a couch cushion or in the linen closet or wherever she last set it down. In the end we made nearly weekly appointments to chat and thus, the narrative became conversation.

Creatives know we are merely stewards of our gifts, that what begins as an outline will, if it has any self respect at all, take control and express itself on its own terms. I thought I was telling the story of Burney's life but I was, in truth, reconnecting with my mother and realizing not only did I love her deeply but that we are as similar as we are different. I still don't always like Burney—I daresay she doesn't always like me either. But somewhere in the bond of story—laughing, weeping, listening, arguing and remembering, I found her. I found my book too and organized the similarities and differences around the primary themes that emerged.

I had coffee with a friend the other day and she said: "You've gotten softer lately." I know she's right and though the vulnerability of the softness is a bit anxiety provoking—I do not, as a rule, expose my belly—I like to think maybe the cold spot in my soul that carries the deep sadness of my fractured family—is in a warming trend.

LEARNING BURNEY

Mother. Some of us get the warm curve of the 'm o', some get the pointy end of the 'e r'. I got the whole word, sometimes writ large, sometimes in pieces but I got her—or at least, I thought I did. Here is Burney, I would have said: smart, hilarious, high heeled, accomplished, affectionate and beautiful. Here is Burney I would have said: meddlesome, critical, high-handed, martyr-prone, performance driven, difficult. All of those things are variously true, but none of that knowledge really offered my mother to me. In good times, I focused on the funny and fun, her generosity and high spirits. In bad times I simply blamed her for my pain and shame, sorting through the strands of our broken family over and over in therapy.

It was helpful, to name the hurts, to allow the sadness to live and to have its say. In the intervening years my mother and I both began recovering from alcoholism and the work of recovery provided further healing and connection in our relationship. We kept in touch on the phone and with visits and developed a fairly easy rhythm of being together. I didn't think consciously about it but if asked I probably would have said I'd gotten as far as I was going to get with Burney. Until the story became conversation.

Conversation takes many forms. Sometimes the exchange is even—words for words, sometimes one person does more listening than talking, sometimes the currency is silence or body language. I often think of my first kiss with my husband Kenny where at last we spoke the volume of our hearts. When the result is an affirmation of the bond, then the conversation, however it transpires, is a success, another stitch in the cloth of intimacy.

Talking with my mother on a regular basis, hearing the stories of her life opened new windows of understanding. First of all, I realized that she too, like me, is wounded. When someone is powerful and confident, it's hard to imagine any broken places—and in Burney's case, she would not readily point them out, preferring to stick to the cliched sunny side and accentuate the positive. But I heard the pain and loss, different from my own but no less crucial to her manner and way of being.

Secondly, I saw how we are alike and not. It is often an unexpected and unpleasant recognition when we say or do something and realize it is a clear echo of our parent. Burney sent me a birthday card once with a woman staring stupidly in a mirror gasping, "Oh my God, Mother???" Inside she wrote, "What could be lovelier?" And I have to say, much of what is similar or pretty much on the money is lovely. I have typically played to the differences—in an effort to separate myself and plant my own flag but playing to differences does not always leave room for empathy. In listening to the shaping events of her life, I realized that I misinterpreted some of her motivations and actions. It's absurd to think I know what's driving another person—though I do it all the time like Karnak the Magnificent giving an answer before the question is even asked. But I don't know—not with friends and acquaintances, not with strangers and not with my mother.

Thirdly, there was no shortage of happy, funny and ridiculous memories. I had swept many of them aside to make room for my brokenness and grievances. Those grievances were real—but so was the rest of it. I needed to be reminded of the whole picture.

In talking with Burney, sorting through a lifetime of her memories, I repossessed my family—not that I had abandoned them—but climbing the tree in its fullness, I began to close the emotional distance feeling grateful for each branch that shaped me—and shapes me still.

The stories are in many ways about everything and nothing, but ultimately categories of identity, family, recovery, body, culture, practice, hospitality and faith emerged. Each category contains the contrasts, the wounds and

6

the great gifts that are mine because of who I am and where I come from.

Not everyone gets a chance to have these conversations with their parents. I had one exchange with my father before he died when in a time of great stress he spoke openly and freely about his life to me between tears and cigarettes for an hour. I keep that hour close and wonder what the conversation might have expanded to given an opportunity. I regret losing the chance to find out but I do know through this experience with my mother that though I got plenty of pointy end with my dad, there's a lot more to the story. . "To know all is to forgive all" goes the proverb. Sometimes when I hear it I think: that's a little neat. But the effort to know and understand has done important work in me, like creating a willingness to lay aside those grievances I like to pick up and pick at, like compassion, not only for my parents but, unexpectedly, for myself too, like the softness that disarms me.

So often when I begin something it is nothing more than a trailhead that isn't particularly well marked. But the best paths are the ones that don't end, that take us deeper into the wild, into the climbs, into the clearings that together become the map of our lives.

IDENTITY

Showing up as ourselves, making peace with ourselves, not too high and mighty, not too low and grovelling, respecting our temperaments while allowing room to expand, thinking about the essential pieces that remain—or emerge—when all else begins to fail.

HUMOR ME

In the middle ages, along with plagues came the Greco-Roman theory of the 'Four Humors'. This was a holistic approach to medicine that identified four temperament types: Sanguine (cheerful, hopeful), Choleric (assertive, hot tempered), Melancholic (depressive, artistic), Phlegmatic (calm, unemotional). The word 'humor' emerges from the Greek word: chymos, meaning juice or sap and each type corresponded to a bodily fluid: blood for sanguine, yellow bile for choleric, black bile for melancholic and phlegm for phlegmatic. The idea was that a balance of all four in an individual produced optimal physical and emotional health. An excess or deficiency of any humor was believed to be the root cause of pain or failure to thrive.

Science and pathology have tossed out the humors as a reliable medical theory but the temperamental aspects remain and have been enlarged and redefined over the years. There are other sources: the equally ancient Enneagram which focuses on the psychological, spiritual and somatic make-up of an individual, the more recent Briggs Myers' personality inventory taken from Carl Jung's typology and the Keirsey temperament sorter. I have no experience with Briggs Myers or Keirsey but I've become a student of the Enneagram. I took the Four Humors test years ago and classified as a melancholic: introverted, artistic, independent, moody, conscientious, reliable, pessimistic and drawn to suffering. The test included a graphic of an 18th century woodcut depicting the melancholic with a massive forehead, sunken cheeks and scowling, thin lips. 'Is this supposed to be helpful' I wondered? But beyond that, the traits were all mine. And the black bile? Yes.

The element commonly associated with melancholics is earth and I rarely miss a day without a trip or two to one of the expansive local parks near my house. I have a need to be close to the ground—to feel it again and again when I'm running or hiking. I fill my pockets and then my house with souvenirs: lichen, moss, discarded nests, rocks, bones, eggshells, I love them for the colors and shapes, the substance and the connectedness to life and death and dirt.

Burney is sanguine. She is outgoing and warm, lively and fun seeking, generous, outspoken and opinionated, happy and sociable. She is optimistic in the extreme and this has not always been welcome or appreciated— at least not by me. In times of deep sadness or disillusionment, when I have only wanted a listening ear, her relentless reminders of all I have to be grateful for strike me as dismissive, insensitive and definitely not good medicine.

But today when my mother called and I asked how she was, she quoted the Doctor's Opinion in the Big Book of Alcoholics Anonymous: "Restless, irritable and discontented." I laughed: "Mom, that's my territory, what happened to little miss sunshine?" She blames the changing world and her inability to find her place in it. She mourns the values, precious to her, that she believes are increasingly lost in this generation. She complains about the casual atmosphere at her church, in dress and punctuality and wonders where the attitude of reverence has gone. The pinnacle of this breach is the accepted practice of bringing coffee into the worship service. She brought it up in her weekly church small group, made up of Baby Boomers and Gen Xers and, not surprisingly got no comment. Burney said: "I guess we'll see if anybody heard me this Sunday." I told her I imagined anybody carrying a Starbucks cup would probably avoid her row and sit some place else.

I think a lot about balance. I know there is truth to types the same way I recognize how grey skies and rain make me feel alive. For years I felt stuck in a temperamental pie wedge, and my own failure to thrive beyond my slice. But there are gifts that come with the work of recovery and my often half-hearted assent to emotional sobriety. One of them is an invitation to spread out among the humors. Some characteristics come naturally to me, like the peaceful, quiet-seeking, rich inner life of the phlegmatic, the talkative, responsive nature of the sanguine and the touchy, excitable parts of the choleric. Other things I have to work at: equanimity, bold action, choosing happiness and sociability, responding rather than reacting, having fun. But practicing these things no matter how badly, also makes me feel alive.

After we hung up it occurred to me that maybe my mother's sour mood is evidence of some balance for her too among the humors: a little yellow bile to beef up her blood, a coating of phlegm, like a layer of cling wrap that makes her want to sit on the couch and watch Flip or Flop on HGTV and the black bile of sorrow that keeps her phone dinging with texts from her prayer chain alerting her to someone in distress and stirring her compassion.

I realize too that my mother's pep talks or silence when I bring up a fresh sorrow are meant to be taken personally but not by me. They are for her. Burney's own life has been scored repeatedly with loss and her insistence on cheer provides pushback against the despair lurking in every corner, despair she would go to great lengths to save her children from. But the language of lament isn't native to her, she's on the other side of the wheel, so she does the thing that feels most comforting and natural to a sanguine and turns her gaze upward and elsewhere.

I used to pray fervently for change, to be someone else, someone nicer and not so moody and volatile. Now I'm thinking it's not change I'm looking for, I've found something worth loving and embracing in every aspect of my temperament. Instead I want to expand.

With that in mind, I pick up the phone and dial. "Mom, I say, you know your 'look on the bright side' bit has stung me more than once. But in a world where free floating anger and anxiety are part of the dispositional atmosphere, your hopefulness is a balm and—I can't believe I'm saying this—but I would miss it—truly miss it—if it was gone. And I would.

ORIGINAL VIGOR

The term codependent emerged in the 1980s as a descriptor of the comprehensive nature of addiction. In AA there are the alcoholic and the co-alcoholics—usually but not confined to family members. Everyone becomes ill; everyone experiences their powerlessness over alcohol. The alcoholic is powerless to stop drinking and the co-alcoholic is powerless to stop the alcoholic from taking that drink.

As the recognition of addiction expanded to include drugs, many treatment protocols adopted the term 'chemical dependency'. Over time the co-chemical dependent term was shortened to codependent. These days, codependence is often over applied to any relational weakness but generally recognized as an unhealthy attachment to another where is there is power imbalance in the relationship and one person has the control.

I've never heard my mother use the word codependent. I'm sure she knows it though it wasn't part of the lexicon of her generation. Maybe it doesn't resonate because she isn't trying to figure out how to regard herself as valuable or how to separate herself from the enmeshment of using others as a mirror of her worth. She simply is herself—fully and happily so. "Hello, I'm Burney" she says—even though she knows her name be misspelled and possibly stretched into Berniece, Bernadette or Bernadine. She puts it right out there, short for nothing, along with good faith she will be welcomed and liked. I have resented that assumption in the past thinking, 'Where's my good faith? I would have thought there was self-esteem to spare in your breast milk alone.'

When I ask my mother the source of that esteem she hops away down a rabbit trail, telling me she likes being well thought of and, apropos of nothing, that she enjoys a good joke. Then she repeats one she learned from the salty talkers in her AA meeting that includes an F bomb. "You didn't think I knew how to say that word, did you?" "No mom, I know you know that word, I just don't quite believe your commitment when you use it."

Back to the ever dimming topic: "Why do you think you have strong self regard?"

She tells me of being allowed to join the church when she was 8 because the pastor decided after interviewing her that though she was young, she understood the seriousness of it. She was asked to sing a hymn in her confirmation service and chose one called: Hold My Hand Dear Lord. She gets tearful telling me she knows through all the ups and downs, poor judgment and foolish decisions, He has never withdrawn that loving hand.

I know faith is the defining substance of Burney's life and has everything to do with the way she views herself and others—but I also know plenty of codependents with a lot of faith. I think perhaps the reason for my mother's evasiveness is she doesn't really have an answer. She has self-esteem and the ability to fully inhabit her space. End of story. But just to be sure, I ask one more time.

She answers: "I have always known that I was loved and approved of." She says her mother used to send her out the door with the gentle admonition: "Remember, you have a loving family and you represent them."

Burney took her mother's words to heart but I wonder if it wasn't that implicit understanding of approval, even more than the declaration of love that shaped her esteem. How many of us have carried an awareness of pleasure in the fact of us, across the family threshold and out into the world?

Ironically, having a healthy self regard doesn't always mean one can pass it on. Because as much as I know my mother's great love for me, I did not leave home with a sense of her approval.

16

Thoreau mused: "I love to see the domestic creatures reassert their native rights—any evidence that they have not lost their original vigor." In many ways, I've spent my life trying to express my original vigor as opposed to representing my family and observing codes of social behavior and presentation that did not fit me and felt superficial, contrived and saccharine. Burney finds comfort and a reaffirmation of who she is in the codes, I found them to be condemning. Therein is the rub. It's easy to bless our children when they follow our lead but learning to validate and appreciate them as they forge a path that is foreign and even threatening is another story. I felt my mother's expectations as rocks in my shoes though I understand she was trying to protect me from rejection. But rejection is an inevitable companion for those of us that break off and out.

In The Book Of Hours, the poet Ranier Maria Rilke writes: "Now you must go out into your heart as onto a vast plain, now the immense loneliness begins." And it was lonely, it's still lonely at times but I emerged from that vast plain with a voice that was mine.

Self is a tricky thing, we cannot forget ourselves if we don't know our value. Thomas Merton said it like this: "To love our "nothingness"....we must repudiate nothing that is our own, nothing that we have, nothing that we are. We must see and admit that it is all ours and that it is all good: good in its positive entity since it comes from God; good in our deficiency since our helplessness, even our moral misery...attracts us to the mercy of God."

I think Burney's first response—after the joke—of God never withdrawing his loving hand from her really is the answer. Because though she could not grant me peace with my own substance, she could and did lead me to the one who would, the source of all self. What a surprise for me to sit fully exposed in the light of God and to find not only nothingness but also belovedness, to find the thing that I have longed for but have not always known: that I was indeed loved and approved of.

FLOATING ON HOT AIR

In a therapists office, an exaggerated sense of self-importance might be noted as a symptom of mental illness but at my house it was part of the training. I ask my mother if she is particularly attached to any of her character defects and she says happily: "Oh, that's easy, grandiosity—though I prefer observing it in others whose lives do not overlap with mine." She is only half-kidding.

The alcoholic community is a teaming pond of ego maniacs with inferiority complexes. We love the sound of our own voices to the point where a lot of AA groups have implemented the 3 or 5 minute rule to keep the talker from hijacking the hour. When time is up, a sign is raised or a chime is wrung, or the meeting chair interrupts and says loudly: "Thank you, that's all".

I was confronted with the sign once when carried away with my own crucial "share" and the memory of it still makes my cheeks burn. But even with the threat of humiliation, I favor grandiosity too and I find new and more subtle ways to keep it in my bag of tricks, like tacit refusal to participate in a conversation I consider frivolous and beneath me.

My mother loves to carp about her fellow AA members whose self-important rants trigger the contempt that accompanies a 'you spot it, you got it' reflex. She mentions Ron who speaks with an affect of drawing out each syllable until the entire room breathes a sigh of relief when he finally finishes the word. He usually wraps up with: "I'm Ron and I'll be here for you. I'm glad you'll be here for me." to which Burney thinks: "Doubtful." She brings up someone she describes as: former member Fred: "Why do you call him former member?" "Because he went back to the place from whence he sprung." "Yes, but that doesn't mean he's a former member." "I know, she says but I just have a feeling he is." "What's your beef with Fred?" "Well, he was an expert on everything whether he knew anything about it or not and he spoke with this superior tone of voice that made it clear he was really pleased with himself.

Then she says: "But I have some experience with antagonizing my fellow members too." Burney describes her first year in AA and a man in an especially large, loud pair of cowboy boots who stomped out the door every time she spoke making it pretty obvious what—or who—was driving him from the room. She said she asked him at one point what his problem was and he said: "I don't like you and I don't like what you have to say." My mother laughed and told him: "That covers a lot of ground but I for one, get a lot out of what I have to say and your big old boots thumping out the door won't keep me from sharing at the meeting." She kept on speaking up and he kept on leaving.

Burney and I both understand that humility is the path to everything we long for, theoretically anyway. We understand that strong personalities and opinions doused in hubris can stir up vengeful responses in those around us. But sometimes neither one of us can help ourselves. I ask her how she picks herself up after a particularly humiliating lapse and she says, "Oh, you know, I have no trouble laughing at myself—but I'm just as ready to laugh at you too. I'm an equal opportunity laugher."

Me, I have a lot of trouble laughing at myself—and that is, I think, the fertile ground where grandiosity thrives. But there's a useful side to an over-amped ego—sometimes it takes a little arrogance and attitude just to get me out the door and into the fray.

Burney says, in truth, her better angels are not too high or low, not seeking special favors but bold in the knowledge that she is somebody in this world and just as deserving of respect as anyone else.

I don't have Burney's boldness. More than once I've admired her for speaking firmly and directly into opposition and even hostility. I don't know that I would call her a peace maker but she definitely holds her truth and has no trouble speaking it. I do not admire that strength, however, when she turns it on me, criticizing a choice I've made with the superior air of church lady. But I turn it on her too. Years ago after what I thought was a good visit she told me her experience of it was a long condescending, one sided conversation where I instructed her in AA protocol. I don't remember what was said but I feel sure she's accurate. That's the thing about grandiosity, I am most prone to it when I am least able to rest in the knowledge of who I am and what I believe. For a long time going home meant packing a chip for my shoulder and something to prove—as if to say—see I took the road less traveled and am better for it—better than you. Holding my space felt like a fight—one that I turned outward—instead of looking within.

My mother is ready to change the subject and says, "You sound particularly loud and harsh today". "Mom, I think you accidentally put me on speaker phone." "Oh, you were filling up the room, like the voice of God" "Ha—just flexing my musculus grandis." "What?" "Grandiosity mom, grandiosity."

PARTY IN A PACKAGE

On my 50th birthday my husband Kenny surprised me with a party. I would like to say I was surprised and delighted—but that's not true. I don't like surprise parties. Kenny doesn't like surprise parties either or any parties in his honor for that matter. Somehow, he forgot he knew me and put together a large gathering with the help of several of my friends. It worked. I was dumbfounded—and immediately stressed.

The room was packed with people from all the threads of my life: music, church, children, AA, neighbors—all standing awkwardly in little clumps around the room. I was the connector and set about frantically trying to get the party started. It was a nightmare. Kenny was so pleased with himself for pulling it off, it was many years before I was able to say to him: "I do not want another surprise party in this lifetime."

I prefer small gatherings where everyone can fit around the table; I suppose all of us have an image in our minds of the way we'd like to be celebrated—or not. I still think now and then of a birthday party in Knoxville my mother gave for me when I was 5 or 6. She says: "I don't remember exactly how old you were but you were very concerned about having a good party so I guess you were old enough to know the difference between a hit and a dud."

I was in luck that year. On a trip with a layover in San Francisco, Burney found costume kits at I. Magnin on Union Square. There were ready made packages with grass hula skirts and Hawaiian bikini tops along with leis and hibiscus flowers to adorn necks and hair. There were kits of pirate costumes with swords, hats and vests. There were party favors too: poppers and chocolate pieces of eight in tin foil. In this case the costumes were the connectors, maybe we should have offered them at my 50th.

Our friend Teenie brought up that party on a recent visit to Knoxville, two of her kids were there and Teenie was so impressed she remembered it too. She said: "Those costume kits were the perfect solution for women on the go."

Burney agreed, "They really were incredible. She turned to me and said: Afterwards you came and wrapped your arms around my legs and told me it was the best party ever. I was so gratified!" What I remember is that all the kids fit around my parents big dining room table.

I ask Burney for more details. She thinks there might have been a treasure hunt and possibly a theme cake because she has a dim memory of a birthday involving brown sugar sand and small plastic palm trees to decorate an icing island. "But really, she says, once you have the costumes down, the rest is easy if you have any imagination." "Which I don't says Teenie." Burney says, "Well, any party with a treasure hunt is going to be a success, especially when children are involved." I might have added: "Only when children are involved." Teenie says: "But you have to hide the stuff and that's hard."

My mother insists it's not that hard and then goes all Norman Vincent Peale: "Well, first of all Teenie, you need a positive outlook." Teenie's not having it: "I know, she says, but don't you beat me up I'm not in the mood." Burney backs off—laughing. She asks if we remember the joke about the little boy who wakes up on Christmas morning to find a pile of manure under the tree and says cheerfully: "I know there must be a pony here somewhere." That's probably in a Norman Vincent Peale book too, I think.

I fall somewhere between Teenie and Burney when it comes to throwing a kid's party. I'm amazed at people who can transform a room or even a chandelier with paper, tulle and streamers, who can take a theme and run with it. I generally preferred destination parties when my kids were kids—like Chucky Cheese where Henry was thrilled to see his hero 'Barney' wandering around the arcade and latched his chubby arms onto the characters legs until Barney shook him off and took refuge in an employee lounge.

Once I branched out and booked Betsy the Clown for one of Lily's parties. Betsy made balloon animals and painted faces. All the girls in Lily's preschool class were there when Betsy arrived in her bright polka dot dress with petticoats. She had her hair in braids, penciled on freckles and big pink lips. The little girls took one look and fled to a bedroom, refusing to come anywhere near Betsy—or her balloons. Lily was the only one brave enough to have her face painted. After that we went back to the Discovery Zone or the Skate Park.

Burney loves a party and is rarely lacking in imagination. When I was a teenager and not at all confident that any of my classmates would want to help me celebrate my birthday, Burney had the idea of serving banana splits for breakfast after a slumber party. She found the long plastic soda shop banana split boats and set up an ice cream bar in the morning. It was such a hit we did it every year after that and all the girls showed up, popular and marginal.

In the last few years I've become interested in the enneagram—a spiritually based personality typing system (or as my friend Kenny calls it, a 'wisdom tradition') around nine descriptions. One of the things that struck me about it initially, in addition to the accuracy of it, is how vastly different we all are. That seems self evident but I guess I thought that while we present differently on the outside, on the inside we are pretty much the same in the way we feel and take in life. Nothing, however could be further from the truth. Some of us move towards, some move away. Some of us take in the world by thinking, others feeling, others doing. There is no right or wrong value attached, it is simply part of the way we are made and formed. The lovely piece is that the strongest groups comprise all the numbers. In that way, we are all connectors.

Each number reflects an aspect of God—love, courage, fidelity and peace are examples. And each number is a reflection of how we are made in God's image and bear that creative stamp. If I had to guess what our friend Teenie's number is, I would guess an 8. Eights embody power and protection—and I think of the hundreds of young people, including me, Teenie has given refuge to at her barn. She taught us to ride and care for horses but more importantly, she gave us a place to be. She is vocal about pretty much everything and her Philadelphia upbringing did not include a soft touch but the city of Knoxville is better because of her generosity and presence.

Burney is not interested in exploring the enneagram for the simple reason that people usually discover their numbers through their sinful, destructive patterns and Burney prefers to discuss her virtues. I suspect my mother is a seven, they reflect the joy and abundance of God which is entirely in keeping with Burney's party personality. There is no stinginess or less is more in her, there is only more is more is more.

I am a four and reflect the depth and artistry of God—though that does not necessarily include the ability to decorate a chandelier.

Rosalind Russell said: "Life is a banquet and most poor suckers are starving to death"

I think perhaps the truth of that has something to do with trying to be who we are not instead of fully inhabiting who we are. The 12th chapter of the gospel of John begins with Jesus having dinner with Mary, Martha and Lazarus. Each one shows up as his or herself: Lazarus, newly raised from the dead is sitting with Jesus at the table, enjoying his company—and perhaps the ability to eat, Martha is extending the hospitality she is now famous for, making and serving the meal, and Mary is at his feet, unknowingly anointing him for burial, massaging essential oil into his rough heels and drying them with her hair.

I wonder how I would have accepted an invitation to 'come as you are' to Jesus. But whether: cooking and serving, engaging him at the table or sitting at his feet, the invitation is the same: whoever and wherever you are, come.

I like the fact that the enneagram is shaped like a wheel, like a round table where everyone has a place and an opportunity to see each other. Teenie's dining room table is round. She knows how to throw a party too—just don't ask her to hide clues for a treasure hunt. And I'll be there—probably on the edges looking for a soul to soul conversation. Burney will be floating about like one of Betsys balloons, laughing and chatting, pumping her happy fizz into the air.

I wish I'd known about the Enneagram at my 50th surprise party. Maybe I wouldn't have worked so hard at trying to connect everyone. Maybe I would have turned my attention to enjoying myself and just let it be. Maybe not. I think that's part of the deal, part of what makes anything good—showing up as yourself—costumes optional.

THE BUSKIN AND THE SOCK

"Your phone's breaking up mom." She laughs and the mouthpiece crackles. She says: "That's not all that's breaking up."

Burney likes to make fun of her aging self—though I suspect privately, it's not much of a riot. She told me the other day she's struggling with anxiety and my brother Paul says her evening visits are more frequent, claiming lonesomeness as she walks in the door with her rummy cube game under her arm. Some people plunge into the helplessness of becoming elderly all at once through an accident or illness. Others take the slow and increasingly unsteady path away from autonomy without taking much note until they keel over or attempt something that was effortless or at least doable a minute ago and realize that the doable is done.

Every day I face my own losses—like the names I can no longer remember and the musical notes I can no longer hit, the smooth elastic skin replaced by age spots and a texture similar to elephant hide. It is also true, at least for me, that though I recognize the inevitability of aging, I'm bowled over repeatedly by the crisis of it. Every indication of my eventual return to the ground arrives with shock waves: "Oh My God..."

Burney is in great health and despite her crone claims I reassure her often that she still has it—because she does—and that she is an inspiration to women coming behind her—because she is. But she is keenly aware of her losses too. She tries to keep the self-deprecating humor going with words and phrases like 'bedraggled', 'woebegone' and 'unexplained tufts of hair' but sometimes, especially at night when the anxiety deepens the shadows in her little house, she is what she is, an old lady in an increasingly strange and fearful world.

Every Wednesday, Burney heads to Sunrise Senior Living where my step father Joe last resided, to teach a bible study. I don't think the current residents have ever once participated in a discussion, or answered her questions so I guess it's more of a lecture than a study. When I have an opportunity to accompany her, I look around at the blank faces and ask her why she bothers since Joe died several years ago. She says:

"I want them to have something to look forward to and who knows, I may wind up here."

This possibility is beyond my imagination.

When my stepfather was moved to the memory care unit at Sunrise, the twice daily visits that broke my mother's heart all over again were tempered by the ridiculous. Joe shared a room with a man named Howard who had had a long, successful career as an importer. Howard and Joe were incompatible; they could not remember what belonged to whom but they never forgot they didn't like each other. In an effort to create something familiar and homelike, Burney delivered Joe's favorite easy chair to their room. But rather than an object of comfort, it became a lightning rod of friction and she would arrive often to find them arguing over whose chair it was. She commented: "Here they were, two captains of industry, reduced to squabbling over a recliner."

Maybe in a last ditch effort to gain the upper hand, Joe formed a mental block against remembering Howard's given name and my mother, thinking it would ease the tension between them, coached him on word association techniques to remedy the problem. Nothing worked and finally, thoroughly exasperated Burney snapped: "Just repeat his name with me Joe: Howard, Howard, Howard!" Joe's response was puzzlement: "Why should I bother when he answers to Walter?"

Eventually the conflict between Joe and Howard escalated to enmity and

Howard was moved to another room. Joe looked forward to potential companionship with his new roommate and was assured by the staff that the man, a doctor, would be a much better fit. But in the flesh he was peevish and gnomelike with a penchant for whining. I think it was around this time my mother arrived one day to find 'help me' scrawled on the wall with a sharpie beside Joe's bed.

Joe took a certain sly pleasure in confiding secret ordeals of kidnapping and torture to Burney. He insisted there was a bomb hidden on the premises and routinely claimed new and intolerable abuses. Once he told her: "I don't like the movie that they're forcing me to watch here every night." Burney thought of the large flat screen tv in the dining room, usually tuned to a station that ran old sit coms in syndication. There were always a few people parked in chairs around the television but most of them were asleep and she was not aware of any organized movie nights. She said: "What movie?" He answered, "Well, I don't know the name of it but it's about a little old man and he's always undressing. I don't like it. I don't see the point." "Joe, that's not a movie, that's your roommate."

Poor Joe, he got stuck living with people he didn't like more than once. Me for instance. He loved my mother and tolerated her children as what he assumed would be a small price to pay. With my sister Windsor, the 'good' one, it was pennies and only an occasional dime or quarter. With me he needed a stack of Benjamins. He had no frame of reference for a broken-hearted, strong willed, displaced ten year old driven by anger, though he gamely tried with his military training to keep me, if not in check, then at least out of juvenile detention. Finally he told Burney one of us—him or me—would have to go. But my step father also eventually forgot he didn't like me, he forgot he had at one time ordered me out of the state of California, he forgot telling me I didn't have a prayer as a musician or a citizen. He and I became friends as he aged and mellowed and that is one of the true gifts of the passage of decades—sometimes the forgetting and what are likely a series of small strokes can sweeten us and give us a clean slate with our former adversaries.

Sid Caesar said: "If you have no tragedy, you have no comedy" And

31

nowhere is comedy more welcome than in the midst of the heartache and suffering of long illnesses, the loss of mind and body, one DNA strand at a time, the inability to remember eating, speaking, knowing and loving. Burney can find humor in just about anything and she passed that on to her children, knowing how much we'd need it.

When all the markers that make us 'us' are gone, what of identity then? I've noticed that aging has a tendency to highlight whatever remains in a person. The kind ones grow kinder and the mean ones get meaner. In Joe's case, after a repressive childhood and depressive adulthood, he entered a kind of James Bond twilight at the nursing home where his worst fears were in many ways realized but also brought out, if not the action hero in him, at least the strategist and gave him something to excite the monotony. He told my mother his plans to evade the kidnappers, outwit the bomb planters and save the Sunrise residents sleeping through the constant danger.

Eventually though, Joe had had enough: enough spy thriller plots, enough roommates who only served as cruel reminders of what he used to have with my mother, enough of Sunrise—and the sunsets too. Surrounded by his family and semi-conscious, Joe breathed in but not out and he was gone. Maybe he saw the Lord, high and lifted up, arms open, maybe he realized he could suddenly run again, maybe he heard the native song of his soul, like the melody of a stream, calling him home.

I looked at the photograph of 'Earth Rise' the other day and thought of all there is to relish and be thankful for on this pale blue dot. But in many ways it is more a comma than a period as we flourish then fade and return to the dust, remarking the brevity of our lives with surprise. I hope for a 'good death' like my father who announced he would not be subjected to a nursing home and a few months later, lay on his bed fully clothed for work one morning and died. But mostly I want a good life, to be here as fully as I can be, to forget my hostilities, to be more kind than mean, to wear both the laughing sock and the sobbing buskin too, the ubiquitous theater symbols of comedy and tragedy. And when the time comes, I hope to let go in peace and step into eternity, no longer bound by time or age but face to face with the God who binds us to himself in love.

FAMILY

Now we begin: fearless, reckless, a seat at the table in a picture not like the painting, Gods footprints in the well of grief, versions of the truth, a box of presents, a sack of burdens, the education that never ends—and always, the love.

NUNC COEPI

Burney has said more than once: "I wouldn't hesitate to offer up my dignity or reputation if the dare sounded fun or promising." She's a nervy girl—that Burney, she carried that attitude 2300 miles across the country with 2 little girls in tow to make us a life in California. I had my own brand of nerve: a cocktail of fearlessness and recklessness—tending to fearless when I had little to lose and reckless when I'd had too much to drink. Fearlessness got me on a stage and eventually to Nashville and a career in music. Recklessness landed me in jail, a hospital, strange beds and, inevitably, fear.

My mother found her nerve on a stage too at the Bijou theater in Knoxville. The Bugs Bunny club offered performance slots before the Saturday movie matinee and Burney stood in line with other little hopefuls in lacy petticoats and bunny fur jackets planning her acapella version of "April Showers". "Did the Bunny club require bunny fur jackets for membership?" I asked. "No, the coats were masquerading as ermine with black patches dyed on randomly but rest assured they were rabbit." I can picture my mother, dramatically dropping her bunny fur to the floor in the heat of her performance. She remembers no such thing--only that she was a self-proclaimed stand out and the hook was in.

My first stage entrance was in the junior high gymnasium for the talent show, playing and singing California Dreamin' on an electric guitar with an amp that was as tall as I was and twice as wide. I have no idea where I got it or who carried it to the stage but I feel sure the amp was the most impressive part of my performance. And the hook was in.

My mother says she stopped short of anything that would take her out of this world permanently but she has a good dose of recklessness in her wake too.

At Sweetbriar College, Burney and some of her roommates read about Minot 'Mickey' Jelke, the "…pudgy heir to an oleo margarine fortune" according to Time magazine. The New York Journal-American had declared him the most eligible bachelor in the United States and my mother in a fit of boredom, suggested writing him a group letter and inviting him to experience the many brilliant minded beauties currently residing at a prestigious girl's school in Virginia. All the girls signed but Burney did the writing and the sending. The Journal-American published it in their letters section with the headline: "A Cry From The Wilderness" and when they discovered it, the reprisal from the school administration was swift. They reminded my disgraced mother Sweetbriar was an institution that prided itself on serious academic pursuit and excellence. Silly, empty-headed, man-crazy behavior like this had no place on the campus and was never to be repeated.

Mickey Jelke himself never responded, fortunately. It turns out he had a taste for young women and later in what was tagged the "Cafe Society Vice Trial" was convicted of two counts of compulsory prostitution in which he masterminded the "Jelke Call Girl Ring". I would have liked to see Mickey Jelke trying to recruit my mother as a call girl. He would have gotten an earful.

My maternal grandfather, Paul Parrott straddled the twin tracks of recklessness and fearlessness too. After his father, a grocer with a small store in Tellico, Tennessee, was murdered in the store by a thief, my grandfather managed to stay in school as far as the fifth grade before going to work selling newspapers on street corners to supplement the family income.

Before the Bijou theater featured the Bugs Bunny club it had a more salacious reputation as a burlesque club and my grandfather landed a better paying job there as an usher. Good pay or no good pay, his mother was

36

horrified and threw him out of the house. He rented a room in downtown Knoxville, continued ushering and sending money home and kept an eye out for a more savory line of work.

When he was fifteen Paul heard of a local doctor conducting interviews for an office boy. He washed, starched and pressed the only suit he owned and went to apply. My grandfather arrived at the doctors office to find a sea of boys and young men, all equally pressed and starched, ahead of him in line. Paul asked for a piece of note paper and a pencil from the receptionist and wrote: "Dear Dr. Alexander, My name is Paul Nelson Parrott. I am the right man for this job and if you don't hire me, you'll regret it for the rest of your life." He convinced the receptionist to deliver the message and got his interview. He also got the job and more importantly, he got Dr. Alexander who became a life long mentor and father figure for him.

A full life summons a lot of nerve. I'm in the twilight hour now having made numerous circuits around the sun. I don't have the knees or the booze for recklessness—but I do find I've come full circle and landed back at the crossroad of 'little to lose' and 'giving up'. Sometimes giving up feels like a super soft sweat suit just waiting for me to put it on but mostly the risk feels small. No ones paying any attention anyway—that's the beauty of aging, the invisibility cloak descends but the give-a-shitter goes down too—offering space to try new things, to risk looking foolish. Because the rules of engagement in this stretch of life are simple: stay engaged.

I think of tenacity as the canopy of my family tree, I assumed my predecessors were all fearless but I'm certain I'm wrong. It's not so much being unafraid—it's doing it anyway, doing it scared. And usually, when people get to 'little to lose'--there's an implied 'left' after little. We are a family that understands loss.

Each day has its own content to attend to, to dwell in. Burney likes to get going with an am radio station playing old hymns, I like to get up in the dark, go out and stargaze before the sun rises. Whatever the ritual, the latin is the same: nunc coepi. 'Now I begin'.

A TURKEY CARCASS
AND A PILE OF DIRTY DISHES

Turkeys, as it turns out, are a favorite 'spirit animal'—probably because they symbolize blessing and abundance. Some of the more enthusiastic animists say things like: "...the turkey spirit animal wants you to be grateful and share". I would think the turkey spirit animal wants you to be vegan. I'm not an animist—though I do have a thing with owls. They show up and show off right when it seems I'm most in need of God, of knowing he's with me, that he loves me. And I do look upon these powerful birds as his emissaries to me.

Turkeys have their own power—those glorious tail feathers fanning out, that prehistoric looking head, the weird wattle that apparently operates like a mood ring and gets redder when they are alarmed or angry and the snood on the end of their beaks that has no known function but swells in males when they strut. These are impressive traits but when I see them in our neighborhood, always in a flock, posse, rafter, mob, gang, clutch, dole, muster (who knew there were so many words for a bunch of turkeys), I think: Thanksgiving!

At Burney and Joe's house, Thanksgiving was often a lightning rod. Burney's family and extended family were a large, noisy bunch, often gathered at my great grandmother's house in South Carolina around a table the length of an ocean liner. My mother considers holidays an opportunity to crowd source and welcomes anyone that strikes her fancy. One year that

39

was the handy man who had been doing repair work around the house. He and my cousin Neel who lived with my parents for several years, hit it off and he invited her to his parent's house where he was living so they could get to know each other. Neel did not fully understand the invitation until the handy man's father answered the door wearing nothing at all but a welcoming smile. He called after her as she beat a retreat to her car saying this was how he relaxed and "Don't be so uptight!" Burney's desire to fill her holiday table remained undampened though and every year she came up with a new list of invites.

Joe was an unapologetic curmudgeon—particularly when Burney was airing out the welcome mat. His idea of Thanksgiving was Norman Rockwell—though I think he preferred the painting itself with everyone in place, stationary and silent. Burney mused, "Well, in all fairness, he was adopted by a childless couple after his parents died and lived in a quiet controlled household from the time he was 5. His mother kept him indoors and occupied to protect him from the threat of tuberculosis and that kind of low key stifled atmosphere was comfortable and familiar to him."

Joe was particularly vigilant about small children, even though he had two of his own. One year he called my sister Windsor who lived across town, to say he and our mother were just having family for Thanksgiving. I suspect it had something to do with her four young boys but it stung her for a long time. On another year, Burney invited new friends that had moved to town recently and knew no one. "Are they bringing those little boys with them?" Joe asked. "Joe, they are their sons—of course they're bringing them" "Absolutely not, Joe said sternly, I can't have all that commotion with those wild hyenas. They'll get Paul and Jennie stirred up and out of control too." "Joe, Burney persisted, they are here and have no one. We cannot be so unkind— and unchristian." But he would not relent, even when my mother played the 'unchristian' card, hoping to guilt him into it. "I like peace and quiet" he said finally. Burney, left with the task of uninviting her new friends said angrily: "Maybe we should just have our Thanksgivings at a mortuary."

Everyone knows the mixed feelings of anticipation and dread that surround holidays, trying to corral expectations and at the same time meet

40

wants and needs for everything from a place to belong to favorite dishes. Someone is always exhausted, someone is usually disappointed, someone inevitably says something offensive and someone else gets hurt or mad, glowing red like the turkey wattle. Burney said one year they attempted an after dinner game that involved teams. Once the teams were assigned Neel immediately got upset. "I'm on the team with the dummies!" she declared and left the table, the dummy team got upset too and left the table, the kids got bored and left the table, Joe said he'd had enough and left the table. Burney alone remained with the turkey carcass and a pile of dirty dishes.

I have a long checkered history with holiday trips home. For years my pattern was to walk in the front door, go directly to the refrigerator and stuff food indiscriminately in my mouth leaving little or no room for the unwanted feelings that arose when I crossed the threshold. I generally stayed food drunk through the whole visit, though now I can't pinpoint exactly what those feelings were—maybe shame over my chunky appearance, maybe the knowledge that not everyone was glad I was there, maybe loneliness and the question, will I ever belong to someone and have my own Thanksgiving table? Probably all of it and then some—who knows all the horses ready to run given a chance.

I still eat too much at Thanksgiving but I've long had my own table—with leaves to expand. I have some of Burney's china and also her penchant for filling that table with people I know well and hardly know at all. I don't even mind the dirty dishes, I like the zen of washing the china by hand and drying it, musing over conversations and what worked in the meal. The carcass is soup.

Last year most of my extended family went to Colorado to celebrate at my sister Windsors house. It was the usual love and drama and it was beautiful—because it was us—me and my family, being who we are and how we are. Anything else would have been nothing but a painting.

THE COINS OF SORROW

The birth of each of my children felt like a small tear in the universe where I unconsciously slipped into a new country of love and vulnerability. Within seconds I understood that here was another person I could not live without. And yet, many of us find we must do exactly that.

My maternal grandparents had four children, 3 girls and a blue-eyed boy with dark blond curls named Michael. Burney has 3 girls and a boy too—my brother Paul who is equally handsome and lovable. Michael was his family's favorite, Paul is ours. I don't think anyone resented giving him the crown—except maybe my sister Jennie who had exclusive rights to 'adorable' until Paul's birth. In Burney's family the older girls viewed Michael as a live doll to fuss over and play with. They were just as wild about him as my grandparents were.

When he was four, Michael began having convulsions and was diagnosed with leukemia, throwing the family into the chaos of uncertainty and dread, facing an illness that was in those days, a death sentence. My grandparents took Michael to research hospitals in Washington DC and Boston but no one could save him. His death left a wound that never quite healed and my grandmother, beautiful, strong and fearless bent under the grief.

My mother felt the impact of Michael's loss too as it threatened the fragile seeds of her new faith. She believed in prayer, she believed there was a God in heaven who loved her and heard her. But her biggest, most important request, to heal her baby brother, had gone unanswered—maybe even ignored. She was eight years old, rarely allowed to leave her driveway un-accompanied, yet the brutality of an unsafe, unpredictable world had come right through the front door and taken over the household.

Burney's maternal grandparents were a study in contrast. My great-grand-father, Edward was a rebellious hard-drinking farmer who raised cattle, pecans and cotton on a South Carolina plantation. My great grandmother, Bessie was refined and genteel, a devout Christian and member of the Pres-byterian church. My independent grandmother, Neel had been closer to her father and did not share her mother's religious zeal. She saw to it that her children were baptized and even sent them to Sunday school every week at First Presbyterian church in Knoxville. But she stopped short of crossing the threshold herself and made it clear to the pastor every time he showed up at the front door to make their acquaintance that he and his overtures were unwelcome.

All of that changed after Michael's death and my grandmother invited that same pastor into her home and her life. She was not motivated by an epiph-any of the spirit but by a desperate desire for reassurance that her darling son was not rotting in a box in the ground.

The Bengali poet Rabindranath Tagore speaks to loves gain and loss in his poem Guests Of My Life, closing with:

After you had taken your leave

I found God's footprints on my floor

Another fine poet, the Englishman David Whyte writes of slipping into the black water of the well of grief and finding the "....glimmering small round coins thrown away by those who wished for something else."

I think often of the lengths I have gone to avoid suffering, for myself and those I love.

I have not lost a child to death but I have lost one to heroin. It is a strange and terrible thing to lose someone who is still alive—something similar maybe to the experience of a phantom limb. I too have fervently 'wished for something else'. And yet it is the very pain I am certain will destroy

44

me that leads me to the vast treasury of darkness where the material world collides with the Holy Spirit offering an unimaginable collaboration and revealing something more than any grave can contain.

In the aching emptiness my grandmother found God's footprints on her floor and the lamp that is the light of the world. Her friendship with Jesus did not fully mend the ragged tear but his own scars made hers easier to carry. In time my grandparents became unlikely pillars of First Presbyterian church and found peace, solace and unexpected gladness to be alive, qualities they were able to share with others in similar straits.

My oldest daughter, Rebecca is never far from my thoughts when I visit my mother. Becca lives in San Francisco and Burney lives in Petaluma, 40 miles north of the city. Once in a blue moon I'll manage to make contact with Becca and even see her briefly.

The visits are hard. I have only the smallest glimpses of my girl, the rest of the time I'm talking to an active addiction that is wily and volatile with deception and self-pity. On my last visit I spoke to my mother twice of the despair I felt of ever having Becca as more than a rumor in my life and each time Burney was silent. I won't say that the silence didn't hurt—because it did. I had hoped for comfort and encouragement, but Burney knows that sometimes our biggest, most important prayers are not answered—at least not the way we long for. I think that's one of the reasons she is loathe to step into the well of grief. Maybe she feels like she would never get out.

Many of us wrestle with confusion and disbelief over the goodness of a God who does not prevent tragedy and loss. But I know that with every prayer begging God to bring my child home to me, what I've been given instead is God himself like an unending supply of those small round coins that, if received, make the loss easier to bear, deepen my connection to a suffering world and shine brightest when tempered by the salt and grit that can only be found at the bottom of the well of grief.

THE EYE OF THE BEHOLDER

How do we tell our stories without telling our version of someone else's story? We don't. At least not when the 'someone elses' are family members and have everything to do with the shape of our stories.

I had an agent who told me her first thought when I handed her my opening chapter to a memoir was: 'Great, just what the world needs, another memoir.' But when she read it, she liked it and pitched it. The upshot was, like it or not, the world got another memoir. Little Black Sheep was published in 2013, the story centers on addiction recovery, coming to faith and the extreme challenges in my family of origin.

My father died in 2002, granting me a little freedom in describing my relationship with him. My mother however is very much alive and I knew there were passages that she might not only take issue with, but would disagree with entirely.

Truth is truth in the eyes of every beholder. I learned that from a wise therapist years ago when he pointed out that in conflict it often doesn't matter who's wrong and who's right. St. Francis asks in his prayer that he become an instrument of peace. He says: "Let me not so much seek to be understood as to understand." All of us bring our experience, our internalizing and our faulty memories to the divided table. In some ways, writing Little Black Sheep was an attempt to understand as much as anything. By the time I sat down to write it, I had been in a long season of relative peace with Burney and I didn't want to disrupt that.

I decided the best peacemaking tactic with my mother would be to include her, so I sent her the galley proofs six months before they went into production. I told her that anything she could not abide I would omit. Then I waited.

Burney and I talk frequently and in our conversations she never mentioned the manuscript. Finally after a couple of months I said: "Mom, have you read the book yet?" "Well honey, I've just been so busy." She had, in fact, been quite busy dealing with an impending move and my stepfather's failing health. I said, "I understand, I just want to make sure you have a chance to sign off on it before I have to turn it in." "Oh, don't worry, I will." Again, I waited.

A month before my deadline I called her and said, "Mom, you really need to read, we're running out of time." "Yes, yes, I know, I will." Two weeks passed and the phone rang. After a bit of chatting, Burney's voice took on a more formal tone as if she was getting ready to say something rehearsed: "Honey, I've been reading and enjoying your book. I do have one small comment to make though."

I thought o.k., now we're getting somewhere. I said: " No problem mom, shoot." "Well, honey, I need to talk to you about your punctuation." "Mom, there's a copy editor employed by the publisher who will be delighted to deal with my punctuation. That's not what I meant when I asked you to sign off on the book."

The odd thing was I knew by the way she was talking, stiff and vague, that she had probably scanned a few random pages and was calling me with this comment basically to get me off her back. The book went to press and my mother had not read it.

Burney came for a visit later that spring to see my youngest child, Lily graduate from high school. We took a trip from Nashville to our hometown Knoxville to visit family and friends and I said to her on the drive: "Mom, I have to tell you, I'm anxious about the fact that this book is going to be released this fall and you haven't read it. I love you and I don't want to hurt you." She said: "I know that and I know your heart. I do plan to read the book and am actually looking forward to it but I deliberately did not read it in advance". Then she paused for several moments before saying: "I wanted you to have your say, your way."

Selfless generosity is rare enough but few of us dive directly into the red zone of personal risk and let others broadcast the things that we would just as soon keep to ourselves. When my mother did read my book, published and on bookstore shelves, she told me she thought it was wonderful—and horrible. She is a woman devoted to making a good impression and I can't imagine what it cost her to step back, to let me fully express my own experience and pain. I often think that it is good to rack up debts in life that we cannot repay and this one certainly qualifies. But maybe we can pay them forward. My daughter Lily's first published poem in a literary journal was called: 'Tell My Mother I Tried.'

UNPACKING CHRISTMAS

At the close of 1964, Burney was packing for a cross country move from East Tennessee to Northern California. She calculated that in order to start her job on time in January, the best day to leave would be Christmas. Christmas Day, where expectation and acute disappointment are just as likely to be under the tree as the contents of our lists. I sit in rooms regularly where seasonal anxiety is an ongoing topic beginning around mid-November and mounting steadily through December. Shopping lists, too much month, too little money, too many gatherings, too much over serving, not only of food and drink but also ill advised comments. All of these poke gaping holes in the peaceful ideal so many of us carry in our heads and knock ourselves out to try and make true.

I was nearly seven years old when we moved to The Bay Area. I had adjusted more or less to my parents divorce. I knew I would see my father on Wednesdays and every other weekend. I knew I would get to ride in his convertible out Chapman Highway to the Golden Arches for McDonald's hamburgers and french fries and maybe go to Dipper Dan's for black licorice ice cream.

I also knew my neighborhood by heart, roaming it as I did after school and on the weekends. I knew the houses I was welcome in. and the moms that would fix me a sandwich. My extended family was a constant presence in Knoxville and Sweetwater and my best friend, Leslie was right down the street. I belonged in Knoxville. Though it was the third largest city in Tennessee, it felt like a town—my town.

We left our home on Yorkshire Drive Christmas afternoon, after my father had driven away weeping, after Mama D. and Papa, my grandparents had said goodbye with assurances of 'wonderful adventures ahead', after Dorothy our housekeeper had heaved herself into the car farting.

I did not realize that moving from Tennessee to California was in essence, time travel or that I would have zero frame of reference for a society that was 15 years ahead of anything in my experience--I hadn't even seen the ocean yet. But I knew enough to know I had lost my place in the world long after the city limits disappeared from the rear view mirror.

I have viewed Christmas with a strong dose of mistrust and suspicion ever since. In California, December represented mounting losses--like snow and cousins. My father sent boxes upon boxes of expensive clothes and jewelry meant for the ingenue he hoped I would miraculously become. "He's shopping for himself." I complained to my mother. "Isn't everyone? she said, And besides, he's doing his part to keep the economy afloat."

One year I was caught stealing in a San Francisco department store and after insisting I confess my crime at church during the time of 'sharing', Burney told me I would have to return my Christmas presents. I can't say I was sorry to see the bright purple poncho go—my dad's Neiman Marcus idea of concession to my hippie aspirations.

I think of my daughter Rebecca's second Christmas when my father fell into a shopping blackout for his first grandchild and arrived in California with the boxes to deliver them himself in one of his brightly colored holiday sweaters. Becca had been primed with Santa Claus stories and when she heard the bells on Christmas she hit the stairs nearly head over heels. But on the landing she stopped short, gaping at the blinding display and burst into tears.

I am so aware of how a box of presents wrapped in expectation becomes a sack of burdens—I think Becca knew that too on some level. I am also aware that the sad memories are not the only memories I have.

Burney loves Christmas--the planning, decorating and cooking. One recent year someone sent me a picture of her heating china plates with her hair dryer, before dishing out the feast she'd managed to pull together in her tiny kitchen and I thought of all the Christmas meals she'd served up through the years, all the roast beef and Yorkshire pudding. She had more counter space then and a double oven but no less love. I think of setting the table, singing Christmas carols, wrapping presents in my room, gifts that I'd either made or saved my babysitting money to buy and I remember the love. My sister and I, at odds the rest of the year (I have a clear memory of chasing her with a pair of scissors) woke up early and played cards until my stepfather rang sleigh bells to call us downstairs. And I remember the love.

Yes, holidays are often lightning rods of friction, yes Christmas is a man-made celebration that we've turned into a display of excess, yes hurt and disappointment have a seat at the table too but there are also the notes and gestures of affection, the gifts that surprise and delight, the feasting—not only of food but of the way we are together, the way we connect—maybe just for a moment but those moments linger now.

I used to take my kids every December to drive by a house boasting 100,000 lights. It was so popular the owner set up designated parking and I imagine it would have lit up google earth as a fiery ball. Every year there was a new snowman, reindeer or angel added to the mix and I have to say, just looking at it was exhausting as I added up the labor. Later I read in the paper that the owner started it after his teenaged son died and I saw the whole thing differently. I imagined him easing his sorrow and loss one strand at a time, delighting children and parents alike. Maybe he truly was aiming for a fiery ball that could be viewed from outer space—or heaven— as if to say—we are here and we miss you.

I find solace and delight in decorating too. Some years I get a little amped and do two trees inside and several more outside. Other years are more subdued but I rarely pass a year without hauling the Christmas boxes up from the basement.

In his poem, The Angel, Rilke writes:

"Give his light hands nothing of your burdens to hold
else they will come to you at night to test you with a fiercer grip
and go like some raging thing through your house
and seize you
as though they'd created you and broken you out of your mold."

I do not regret my ambivalence towards Christmas because it left an empty space in my soul that eventually filled with Advent. I love to get up early each morning in December, light the candles and the tree and sit in silence. I contemplate the incarnation, the gift of Jesus, the coming new year and all the ways I might be seized and broken out of my mold.

SEE SPOT, IT'S OK TO BE DIFFERENT, SPOT

When I google Pepper I get spice images and a link to a site exclusively for bell peppers with an emphatic banner: "The world's healthiest food!" Down the list is W. H.Pepper Pre-School, a model of early education begun in Petaluma, California by Mr. Pepper in 1894 and inspired by the German Educator, Frederick Froebel who gave us kindergarten.

Pepper schools focus is an integrated curriculum with options in music, art, language, science and movement. "See Spot Run" is replaced with "It's OK To Be Different" and implemented in an atmosphere with a mission of affection, respect, mutual understanding and peace. Not at all like the wild, wild west in a cyclone fence that was my elementary school playground. Burney sent my sister Jennie there when she was four and Jennie remembers it as a happy experience except for the time a kid hit her in the head with a hammer in the tool shop play area. He, apparently had not read the mission statement.

In the mid-70s, Pepper Schools model of equality was considered progressive if not revolutionary. Teachers stepped down from their lofty perches of absolute authority and offered choices, a sympathetic ear and even their first names to students. My mother was skeptical about certain elements of the new pedagogy. She told the head of the school that children calling adults by their given names was unheard of in her native Tennessee and since they still headed south for visits, she was uncomfortable with such familiarity. They settled on attaching Mr. or Miss to a teachers first name. Also, the reflective style of 'active listening' or repeating back to the child their words to let them know what they said had been heard and heard correctly seemed excessive and unnecessary. Burney told the headmistress: "I'm pretty certain that I get what my children are saying to me—and that they get what I'm saying to them."

Nevertheless, in an effort to reach across the aisle, my mother attended a lecture at the school by a visiting educator speaking on current trends. He demonstrated active listening:

Child: "I'm excited because we are going to the park!"

Adult: "You are excited about the park today!."

Or:

Child: "I'm sad because Cindy's puppy died."

Adult: "Cindy's puppy died and you are sad."

It sounded simple enough, what could possibly go wrong?

One grey morning, Jennie thumped down the stairs in her nightie, collapsed in a sullen heap at the landing and moaned: "I can't go to school today. My head hurts, my legs hurt, my whole body hurts and I have no friends." Here was an empathic opportunity just waiting for employment! Burney responded gravely: "Your head, your legs, your whole body hurts and you're sad because you feel that you have no friends."

Jennie stared at my mother and cried: "Rub my face in it will you!" before rushing back up the stairs sobbing.

This set back apparently did not fully douse my mother's enthusiasm for alternate forms of education. She sent Jennie and my brother Paul to the Waldorf School even though it involved a daily commute to another town. Burney said there was a lot to like about Waldorfs classical education style. She particularly loved the inclusion of gardening in the curriculum to teach,

56

as she described it: "…the seasons and orderliness of the world."

Her aesthetic eye was gratified by the high quality of the materials down to the paper stock and the beautifully illustrated books. Lunch bags and boxes were exchanged for hand made baskets, tee shirts with slogans were exchanged for natural fibers and dye classes. The children were greeted with a hand shake when they arrived and sent to their cubbies to exchange their shoes for black slippers.

At Waldorf, students were taught diction, eye contact and projection when speaking in front of the class. These days those things are extra curricular and found in forensics groups, drama class or speech pathology. But to Burney they were and are foundational to getting along in this world. She muses: "You know, I think Waldorf was where I first tasted seaweed" Jennie doesn't remember sampling seaweed but says popcorn topped with brewer's yeast was a staple for snacks and as unappetizing as it sounds.

My stepfather had a business conflict on the initial parents night at Waldorf but Burney said it was just as well. He would have stuck out like a sore thumb in his pin striped suit and barbershop haircut. She described the scene to her conservative husband: "All the fathers had ponytails, buns or even pig tails but none of them wore underwear." "How do you know?" asked Joe "Well, it certainly wasn't my focus but when things are a little loose and out of place, one can't help but notice." Joe made it to the next parent night but was keenly disappointed at the refreshment table. What was the point he wondered, of making a cookie with whole wheat flour?

Burney appreciated both Pepper and Waldorf schools but wasn't fully on board with the whole philosophy of either—particularly the idea of what she described as constant praise with or without merit. She said: "I like to encourage children but the idea of commending a child for everything, even when done poorly doesn't make sense to me."

Trophy culture is alive in the public schools too though. I have the 'star of the week' posters to prove it. I recall swearing loudly as I scrambled to make these elaborate collages in between work, carpool, laundry, sports and meals: "When exactly are my children not the stars of the week?"

I fall somewhere between Burney, Pepper and Waldorf in the praise department. I don't think kids get their security from constantly being told they are special but I don't think a performance based atmosphere is helpful either—personally, I'm still trying to get over that one. I could have used more 'atta' girl and fewer evaluations—sometimes spoken and sometimes merely delivered by a trained eye taking my measure.

Parenting has been the source of deepest joy and deepest anguish for me. What worked beautifully for one child was a disaster for another and I have spent a good bit of my adult life asking forgiveness and trying to accept it for the many failures I racked up. Who among us has what it takes to bring another person to adulthood unscathed? Certainly not me. I am keenly aware that I gave my children as much affliction as affection—maybe not in equal measure but they all got the best and worst of me.

Burney has her own regrets. "I know my children love me, she says, I didn't always deserve their love and respect but they gave it anyway."

I think every child wants to believe the best about their parents. In my case—there's plenty there to love and respect. But the path is an honest one, paved just as clearly with pain and disappointment as with love and nurturing.

That's the real education no head knowledge or book learning, or alternative education can change: that whatever we are doing as parents, we are doing it imperfectly and often in the dark, that despite any mission statement, the playground is still the wild, wild west, that we will devote ourselves to our children but also cause them pain and fall wide of the mark in our interactions with them. As much as I look upon my children as supreme gifts, I look upon them equally as sources of despair that highlight my own controlling nature, intolerance and inadequacy. Maybe God intended it that way, as if he's saying: "Here you go: the bone of your bones, the flesh of your flesh, the joy of your heart, the rock in your shoe, the thorn in your side, the revealer of all that is beautiful and horrible in you. Have fun trying to run the show. I'll be here when you've worn yourself out with your programs and solutions." And he was right there. And he is right here still, teaching me daily the broad strokes and fine points of love in a class that never ends.

RECOVERY

Look! Look! Don't Look! Chasing the velvet, surrender in two acts, learning the words that need each other, losing the ones that don't, the three legged stool that wobbles, secrets along with a tip on the table and the revolution in our souls.

A LITTLE BIT OF HOPE

Burney employs a persistent, sometimes dogged optimism to keep her buoyed on the often churning waters of life. I ask her, "Mom, can you think of a time when you felt completely hopeless?" "Only one, she says, when I realized I was an alcoholic." I am not expecting this and can only respond: "Really? Why?" She laughs and says: "I'm puzzled you would even have to ask me that question."

She has a point. I have the same affliction and I too fully subscribed to the notion that drinking made life not only bearable but worth living at all. Never mind that it was killing me. Giving it up meant any notion of ease and fun would be in the rear view mirror, waving and winking and blinding me, like the party lights I loved to chase. But still. Burney has suffered the untimely losses of her own mother to cancer, a baby brother to leukemia and a sister to, of all things, alcoholism. She has survived a divorce, financial downturns and the death of a beloved husband. All of those cost her dearly and she tells me that though she came very close, she did not lose heart. But her wine? That was something else entirely…

She's not alone. For two years I co-facilitated a monthly group meeting at a sober living house. A mixed bag of residents showed up—usually a different cast of characters from the previous month. There were those diverted from longer jail sentences for possession and prostitution among other things. They were given the option of treatment and took it to get out sooner though not necessarily to get sober. Others were attempting to crawl out of a very low bottom and serious about their recovery efforts. I could usually tell the ones marking time—possibly because they lay their heads on the table and slept through the meeting. My hope for those women was that something would slip through and catch. On my last visit, one said to me, "I don't know about this recovery thing, AA is no fun—and boring." She was one that had been remanded from the county jail, she had lost her children, her house, her freedom and here she was in a place that no one would choose to call home. One might wonder how much fun could possibly be worth all that but when the illness of addiction is active, the answer is always: just a little more.

Burney had reached a joyless, desolate place, knowing she couldn't go on much longer pouring a glass of wine first thing in the morning as she fired up the vacuum cleaner. She was far from wellbeing, far from her family, far from God and about as far from fun as you can get. But the idea of facing any of that along with the mundane chores of life without her gallon jug nearby sent her into a spiral of hopelessness.

Eventually she gathered her courage and spoke into the darkness one evening just after she and my stepfather, Joe had climbed into bed. She confided her heart and her fears, naming them aloud perhaps for the first time and was rewarded for her courage with her husbands snores. Once she got past her initial anger, she decided she would put her helplessness on paper because anyone married to an attorney knows they will generally be attentive to a yellow legal pad. And he was.

My stepfather is not famous for optimism and during his lifetime, tended to dwell with the rest of us melancholics who see the glass not as half empty or half full, but smashed on the floor. My mother did not anticipate that he would offer much to her beyond commiseration but she was wrong. Joe said he was glad for her honesty and told her he thought he had a solution. One of his specialties was hospital law and he happened to represent the only facility in the town where they lived.

Petaluma Valley Hospital had recently designated an unused wing for an early addiction treatment model. In 1983 treatment was hardly part of public lexicon and it was unusual to have proximity and access to an in-patient unit. But here it was right down the road and Joe told my mother it might just be her golden ticket. As it turned out, I wound up in the same wing thirty days before my mothers stint after a trip home for the holidays became a lost fortnight and my family intervened. It was there that both of us began our paths to recovery and hope.

I remember walking the perimeter of the hospital parking lot early on, bloated and morose, thinking of all the never agains in my life: never be a party favorite, never get to have wine with my dinner, never laugh, never write a decent song, never, never, never. My sole sources of comfort were the thoughts that my 2 year old daughter might actually get a mother and maybe I'd lose a little weight. Beyond that things looked grim.

I have a particular affection for the second of the twelve steps from the Big Book of Alcoholics Anonymous: "Came to believe that a power greater than ourselves could restore us to sanity." The first two words are in many ways a full expression of my own sanity recovery as I have gradually 'come to' in nearly every area of my life—first with honesty. I had to admit that I was far more of a party liability than a favorite, that I did not drink wine with dinner, I drank wine for dinner and a vintage bottle could easily be supplanted by mad dog 20/20 mixed with kool-aid if that's what was on the table. I had certainly had many moments of hilarity under the influence but the laughter was often at my own expense and forced, as if to say, "Look, look, look!" and then "Don't look!" And the days after? They weren't funny at all. I honestly didn't know how my songwriting would fare, but I did know that if I kept drinking through shows, falling into equipment and losing my voice in the first 20 minutes, I wouldn't have a venue for my songs anyway.

My mother has forgotten her sobriety date but she's well into thirty years. She says she got her joy and optimism back as soon as she swallowed her pride, went to a meeting and accepted the silver chip that signals the desire for a new way of life. I ask her what she does to keep her hope alive and she says: "Oh you know, the usual."

63

For Burney, the usual is faith in a loving God and filling her life with people, particularly children who are ready sources of light and energy and provide a welcome distraction from the vagaries of old age. Then she says, "But you know, if I'm really down, the age old remedy of getting my mind off myself and helping someone else never fails."

I suppose both of us have redefined the word 'fun' in our lives. I tend to serious, solitary pursuits and have to be intentional about setting aside time for pleasure. My husband, Kenny tells me television doesn't count—but he's wrong. The thing that I do know is that drunken fun and sober fun are opposites. In my alcohol and drug fueled sprees, fun was about absence: absence of fear and inhibition, absence of restraint, absence of difficult feelings, absence of difficult me. Sobriety offers a mellower fun that is wrapped up in presence, in good company and conversations from the heart, in the laughter and tears that accompany our daily bread.

I do not have to ask my mother if she is having any fun these days. When I finally get her on the phone, she's usually whispering over laughter in the background that she'll have to call me back, she's at a party or her small group or her cutthroat rummikub game at the senior center. We have re-placed the despair of our affliction with a little bit of hope and it turns out a little bit of hope is a lot of hope—more than enough, to inhabit a day. It is the tip of infinity, the unseen world of God who takes fragments, like the leftover bits of loaves and fishes, and fills them with himself.

For this reason, everything, particularly the things I think are worthless or will cost me most and give back the least, becomes the potential source of greatest treasure. Unlike Burney, I am no optimist. I side with Joe and the rest of the melancholics of the world. But even on days when tears feel inevitable, I know that I have a message of life in me to carry and a little bit of hope keeping me upright and mostly sane that I am meant to pass on. I tell God: "You know the day I realized I was a hopeless alcoholic? Turns out—that was a pretty good day."

BREAD WORTH SHARING

I tell Burney the topic is tolerance. "Hmm" she says. "Maybe you should change it to fed up". I ask her to list the things she is most intolerant of these days, thinking that she will launch into a commentary on the state of the world, the deplorable condition of the political framework, terrorism, pandemics, mass shootings, the economy, the racial divide, abuses towards women, all things she has plenty to say about on any given day.

Instead she says: "Grunginess". I should have known. If Burney had been a Miss America contestant, her version of a wish for 'world peace' would have been a wish for 'world grooming'. She is, after all, someone who dresses and accessorizes for yard work.

She is quiet for a moment and then adds, "Oh and poor cooking. Anyone can follow a simple recipe, there's no excuse for a bad meal." She adds to that her dismay at people who bring a tub of commercial chicken salad or an unopened bag of greens along with bottled dressing to a potluck. "Whatever happened to making an effort?"

I point out that many people do not have her prodigious talents in the kitchen and lack confidence. Or maybe they're busy. She says: 'That's no excuse.'

Cooking skills can be learned to a certain extent but a meal is elevated to an art form with an intuitive sense of touch, timing and proportion. My mother has that savvy and is a deft, enviable cook. Though she insists that anyone can follow a recipe on their own, I have memories of her snatching biscuit dough out of my hands telling me I was pawing it and would end up with door stops.

The Oxford Desk dictionary defines the word tolerate as: "Allowing the existence or occurrence of without interference." The big book of Alcoholics Anonymous declares: "Love and tolerance of others is our code." The word 'tolerance' appears elsewhere in AA literature 15 times and is foundational to our success in sobriety; we are people who displayed boundless tolerance for our own substance abuse but little to none for the opinions and behaviors of others. In our fellowships we learn to accept and even appreciate those behaviors and opinions spouted by people from every high and low of society, comprising every belief, every perspective, every personality type and every tic on the human scale. If we are persistent and diligent at the work of recovery we eventually turn that acceptance towards ourselves, then carry it into our "…sometimes deranged family lives" (Twelve and Twelve step 12, pp 111, 112) and beyond.

At the close of many meetings, AA members gather in a circle, hold hands and recite either the Lord's Prayer or part of Reinhold Niebuhr's Serenity Prayer:

God, grant me the serenity to accept the things I cannot change
The courage to change the things I can
And the wisdom to know the difference

And there is no greater wisdom than the recognition that the courage to change the things I can applies to me and only me.

Burney keeps track of newcomers to her morning meeting and makes a point of gravitating towards them, particularly those that are unwashed, downcast and unable to make eye contact. She welcomes them, she squeezes their hands at the close of the prayer, urging them to 'keep coming back'; she learns their names and greets them if they return. She abides the loose talkers, the cross talkers, the grandstanders, the newly sober and the not yet sober. In the rooms of AA, she is kind and full of forbearance. It is everywhere else that she occasionally slips in the 'without interference' department. I can't really fault her—though I do—but I too am rarely short on critical thinking—about me, about you, about anything and anyone. But take away the tolerance and the love that leavens it into bread worth sharing and there is there is no good will or peace to be found.

I learned this the hard way with my beloved cousin Neel who tumbled down a rabbit hole of fear, insecurity, depression and displacement on the back end of middle age. She could not rise above it—she couldn't remember daylight, and wept in despair through every conversation we had. I say conversation but on my end, it was an incessant pep talk, urging her to do this, that or the other thing to pull her life together. When that didn't work, I just fell silent. But it wasn't tender, supportive silence, it was the kind of recoiling muteness that causes a person like me to emotionally flee the premises, fearing I might catch the misery if I don't interfere, if I just let it be. At one point Neel lifted her head and gazed at me long enough to say: "I can feel your disdain."

If I was going to catch anything, thank God I caught those words and let them bring me to my own despair. Here was someone I loved like a sister that needed nothing from me but compassion and I wouldn't or couldn't give it.

Over time Neel recovered and found purchase on happier ground. She forgave me my failure to love her well, though I don't know that I ever fully forgave myself. Once I saw the heartlessness of it, the damage, I wanted to change—and though I don't know that I'm any more free of the intolerance that communicates as contempt, I do catch it quicker. And I am far more liable to turn to God with a word: help.

I come by my intolerance honestly, it's a given for people with my disposition and personality type. What I wasn't born with, I learned on the knees of and under the critical gazes of my parents. Though they both had great capacity for kindness, they were equally liable to sharp tongues and eye rolls over someone else's looks, behavior, opinions etc. etc.. etc. I remember discovering the word 'sarcasm' was derived from the Greek 'sarkazein' meaning: to tear flesh. No surprise there—that was a primary form of humor for us.

Freewheeling through the first twenty-five years of my life did not include much of an effort at loving or tolerating anyone. How could I? I had no love or tolerance for myself.

The great beauty of 12 steps is taking them beyond theory into action and discovering that even though I'm often not very good at it, the spiritual deterioration that accompanies addiction begins to transform and I have an ever deepening desire to love and let love, to live and let live.

I used to wonder why the Big Book paired love and tolerance together as a code. It felt like putting warm colors with cool. I understand now that without tolerance there is no love and without love, the tolerance is grim. They need each other.

Burney threw a birthday party for a friend once who thanked her and then delivered a list of dietary restrictions similar to the Overeaters Anonymous grey sheet. But after a few deep breaths my mother gamely accepted the challenge—though she said she snuck a tiny bit of butter into one dish to make it palatable. Cake was out of the question but I heard the party was a success because whatever sweetness lost in the absence of flour, dairy and sugar—was found and leavened by the love and tolerance around the table.

THE FORBIDDEN WORD CLUB

My mother, my sister Windsor, my cousin Neel and I instituted a forbidden word club. The only requirement for membership was a list of expressions we mutually hated and tacit agreement never to speak them.. 'Moist' comes to mind along with 'commode' (a favorite noun for my grandmother); 'soiled' is another. Over the years we added and subtracted—we also attached conditions. For instance: you could only use the word 'soupcon' if you were French, or at the very least fluent in French. Burney is neither of these things but she loves to fill her discourse with 'bon mots', as she would say. Still, I would rather hear her say: 'soupcon' than 'dollop'—another word that gives me the creeps.

Next, perfectly reasonable words could not be reworked as self-important descriptors. For example: 'curate' could only be used in relation to art or museum collections. Any pompous reference to curating ones offspring, groups of people, musical recordings or compositions was strictly off limits. Also—the generally accepted terms: caring and confrontation were never to be united under any circumstances unless one was interested in a fist fight.

I have a Dilbert cartoon on my refrigerator in which the conversation between two office mates goes like this:

"Do you mind if I give you some advice?"

"Not at all. Do you mind if I roll my eyes, sigh deeply and dismiss your advice as if it came from the village idiot?"

"I might mind."

"Well then, let me give you some advice...."

I am a 'know it all'. Burney is a 'know it all'. Both of us have learned the hard way that not only words but entire sentences deserve striking at times in the interest of good communication and rapport. I tell her that silence—and minding our own business is far more golden than we could have imagined. She responds: "How boring." I mention a Proverb (18:6) that leapt out to me when I first read it: "With his mouth, a fool invites a beating." How many wars, I wonder, started with a word.

In Alanon, a twelve step group for the family and friends of alcoholics, people often show up for meetings initially thinking they will be given tips on how to get the drinker sober. What they hear is that the alcoholics recovery is out of their hands and, in fact, none of their business, that they are their own qualifiers for membership because they have been affected and distorted by the illness as well and that Alanon offers personal recovery-period. For those that stick around and—most don't—a new world of freedom, peace of mind and meaningful pursuit presents itself. The often surprising piece of it is when a hands off approach and a few healthy boundaries are adopted with the alcoholic or addict and replaced with loving, compassionate detachment, the users often take responsibility for their own lives, get help and get clean and sober.

When I first heard the phrase: "loving detachment" I was confused. My only experience of detachment was the decidedly unloving silent treatment delivered by my father over any rule infraction. And every silence was pointed and brimming with message. My sister told me once he didn't speak to her for sixty days when she accidentally broke one of his prized— and easily replaced—crystal highball glasses. The idea of a silence that was benign and even supportive, regardless of any difference of opinion was a new language for me. Here was a familiar space along with an invitation to inhabit it in a novel and even frightening way. Because loving detachment dispenses with expectation, manipulation and, in many ways, the hope of getting what we want from the other person. Often, in the quiet, I find that I am overwhelmed with grief, for what I'm longing for, for what

70

I've longed for all my life, for what may never be.

I cannot say that I have achieved mastery or even consistency with this detachment business. It's a tall order to stay out of someone else's choices when I am often deeply affected by them. But if I focus my options and actions around my own life, I find I have plenty to keep me busy and that the end result is a healthier, more honest exchange all around—along with an atmosphere swept clean of discord.

Burney has eased her way to diminishing her vocabulary of opinion too though only recently and not entirely. Too bad she hadn't adopted this approach in my drinking and drugging days, we could have avoided some knock down drag outs and left a whole lot of painful words unspoken. Detaching involves more death of self than most of us would like to embrace—ever—and sits on an unstable learning curve. My sister told me of a time when our mother came to visit for a few days. Burney watched her walk in the room one morning and said: "Honey, I think you would look so much better if you would put on a little make-up. You have a lovely face but we all need a bit of assistance here and there." Windsor looked at her and said: "Mom, it's 6:30."

I don't think of myself as a particularly meddlesome person—but I imagine no one prone to trespassing in the affairs of others thinks of themselves as anything other than helpful and caring. The daily deaths: to my opinion, my 'rightness', my good advice are low, very low on my list of enjoyable pursuits. But living well and loving well are high on the list and unwanted counsel or criticisms are immediate deterrents.

So it goes—the effort to tame the tongue, the prayers for a sentry of peace at the door of my mouth, the intention to expand the forbidden word club to include anything that invites a beating or unnecessary division and the willingness to enlarge my vocabulary with the language of understanding and acceptance. Most of the time though, when I feel something rising up, the word that comes to mind and helps me stand down is: yield.

KICKING THE GOADS

"Recovery is a three legged stool…" goes the saying. One leg is principles or the 12 steps that we work and work again. One leg is the fellowship: meetings and regular contact with other members of our community. One leg is our Higher Power: the God of our understanding and the force behind our sobriety and restoration. Break or remove a leg and the whole thing falls. Or does it? No one among us follows the prescription to the letter—or if they do, they run the risk of being an intolerable pit boss. We are a group that focuses on the slogan: "Progress, not perfection."

Sponsorship is a fundamental part of 12 step recovery. A sponsor is typically someone of the same gender who has worked the steps and is willing to make themselves available to walk through recovery with another person. When looking for a sponsor, we're told to listen to people in meetings and to ask someone that speaks honestly and is focused on their own program, someone whose content offers hope and a manner of living that we ourselves would like to adopt. A sponsor is not an authority or an instructor, we're a fellowship of equals who have discovered that when one person listens to another and responds openly and truthfully from their own experience, recovery gains a heartbeat.

When I first came into AA—I didn't go to meetings much, having a fear of groups where I had no status or leverage. I don't recall ever asking anyone to be my sponsor and if I did, I doubt I ever called her. When I returned to the program after my relapse, I returned in full, meaning, I had a new and unusual willingness to follow the suggestions. Since then I've had two tremendous women speaking into my life as sponsors over the years, giving me the crucial benefit of their perspectives. Addiction and all the companion family illnesses that stem from it is marked by distorted thinking and denial. Someone well-versed in AA practice and literature but unrelated to me and uninvolved in my affairs can help clear the Johari window pane that represents my blind spots, those things about me others can see but that I am ignorant to. I've had plenty of valuable individual and group therapy over the years but nothing has changed me like the habit of step work with a sponsor. Those steps, done repeatedly have led to transformation.

At the last meeting Burney and I attended together, she referred to me as her sponsor. 'This is news' I thought, I don't recall her ever asking me to sponsor her—or even to ask my opinion on her program practice. In truth, I think Burney offered me up as her beard. She had a sponsor initially whom she said was helpful but after the woman moved away, Burney never replaced her. She's a one and done kind of gal. She says she sponsored a few women early on but they moved away too and she let it go after that. She says: "I don't think I had the enthusiasm for the long haul with people, I was already doing that with a husband and children, I didn't want to take on anyone else."

My mother had a relapse too, shorter than mine but long enough to convince her she had lost her joy and was not going to be able to locate it in her wine bottle. After less than a year she swallowed her pride, returned to the meetings, introduced herself as a newcomer and picked up the silver chip that is tactile evidence of our desire for a new way of life. That was over 30 years ago and to my knowledge Burney has never looked back. Nor has she missed many days without a meeting. Nor has she gotten a sponsor. Her absorption of AA has happened in the group, hour by hour, day after day. She may not work the program as written but somehow her stool still stands.

I ask Burney if she's ever formally done the steps in order and she answers: "Yes but I was initially very negative about the steps, I thought they

74

were stupid. Actually she continues, it was you that convinced me they were worth the time and effort." "Were they?" I ask. "Yes, but I never felt the need to do them again." No surprise there either but though Burney may feel the steps were merely a bit of unpleasantness to clear from her plate—I do know she lives them.

I'm the opposite. I have lapsed in meeting attendance periodically over the years but my focus on step work has not wavered and I consistently engage them not only for my recovery but also with others for theirs. I love having a sponsor, I love being a sponsor too and the perspective gained from sitting with another woman as she wrestles with the complexities of learning to live without alcohol and the work of honesty and self awareness. I do love the fellowship too and consciously try to up my meeting attendance but sometimes I love solitude more—so it's an ongoing effort to get myself out the door and into the room. Somehow my stool is still standing too.

I'm grateful that our bylaws are presented as suggestions. Probably because where we alcoholics are concerned, skittish as racehorses, ears twitching, any rule will be met with outright rebellion and refusal. But suggestions are gentle reminders that maybe we don't know everything, that maybe if we did we wouldn't be sitting in a Sunday school classroom under fluorescent lights, bent and broken. Every year I seem to employ another program suggestion as if it had just been presented to me, though I've heard them all since day one. But honestly, the day or days something is said to me and the day I actually hear it are rarely the same day.

In the end, the thing that makes recovery happen, the thing that is the culmination of all those suggestions, is somehow it becomes our way of life. And not just a prescription for wellness— our recovery, our friendships, our service, all of these become precious—even sacred to us.

Burney told me yesterday: "I sang at the meeting this morning, not for long. They were all transfixed." "I bet they were I said laughing—what did you sing?" "All The Way My Savior Leads Me. Then I told them I certainly hoped that their higher power was a savior because that's what I needed and that's what they need too."

AA tradition speaks directly to leaving our specific beliefs or religion outside the meetings. People must be free to define their higher power on their own. In my group there are people from nearly all the major religions, all denominations and also atheists who look upon the strength of the group itself as their higher power. Burney knows this but sometimes she kicks against those goads and goes preacher on her group. I don't think anyone pounces on her though, they love her dearly, chalk it up to her 'elderly' status and take her as is. Many of them tell her that her words and presence mean the world to them—another reminder that God uses all of our humanity—including the sand and cracks in the clay—to bring life to his creation.

My mother will be a vital part of her fellowship as long as she is alive, she may not keep the rules but, honestly, alcoholics are notorious for insisting the rules don't apply to them and that attitude doesn't necessarily change in sobriety. We all show up as ourselves and carry the flame on any given day with what we've got. And fortunately what we've got is grace.

TELL IT LIKE IT IS

I used to drink martinis with my father. Now I go to AA with my mother. At one meeting the topic was secrecy and when Burney spoke up I tuned in. I grew up with the impression that my mother had been a consultant when the propriety rules were written, that she had no reckless youth, no shadowy past and no secret worth keeping. My aunt Marion assures me: "Everybody thinks of Burney as the do-gooder in the family, always looking out for the poor and pitiful, but there's another side of her." I hope so, I thought.

Burney told the group she'd buried something so deep she forgot it and it was no small surprise to her when it popped out of her mouth over coffee with two AA buddies. Her companions, a psychologist and a clerk at JC Penny reacted very differently. The psychologists jaw literally dropped, unnerving my mother who said sharply: "Don't look at me like that! You're a therapist, you're supposed to look impassive and unaffected and say, 'hmmmm' in a reassuring manner."

The other friend laughed and said: "Oh Burney, that's nothing! Let me tell you what I did—it's much worse—not even in the same category." She repeated it to my mother who said: "You're right, that is worse." The women began laughing and to my mother's great surprise and relief, they moved on like it was no big deal. And suddenly it was—no big deal.

A secret shared is a burden halved—something like that. In addiction culture we remind ourselves often that our secrets keep us sick and isolated. We tell them to stay sober. We tell them to be free. We tell them, not so much to make them known but to make them right if we can. If we can't we can at least take responsibility and deflate them in the telling. My mother left her shame and regret on the table along with a tip and walked out the coffee shop door.

I am not nearly as judicious and compulsively tell pretty much everything indiscriminately. I have a need to confess, usually to the wrong people—like my mother—who could not hear my crimes without mentioning God's terrible judgment aimed directly at me. I don't know why I chose to unburden myself with Burney, I knew how she would react. In a way, I think I set her up to deliver the condemnation I felt was due me. That's another aspect of telling secrets—it's unnecessary and cruel to saddle someone with information they do not want or need and cannot help but react to.

I continue to be more or less a literal open book, having detailed many of my 'secrets' in a memoir. But I do have the added discernment prayer provides of understanding when circumspection and a single trusted ear are the better course of wisdom and when to let truth lie on the table for people to take or leave as they will.

Burney surprised me a few years ago, standing in front of the women at her church, generously giving details of her story others would have left out. She mentioned her lingering sadness over an abortion she'd had between marriages and as I sat watching her discard her white propriety gloves one finger at a time, I thought of how she had walked through my own unplanned and terrifying pregnancy with me, day after day, week after week. I made the choice to carry and keep my baby, Burney chose differently. Both of us paid a price for our choices. I had my beloved daughter and would do it all over again but the abandonment she carries in the absence of a father and my own addiction instability cost her dearly and contributed to her instability and addiction. Choice is an often terrible but precious gift, and all of us must carry each one we make. Our choices can also inform our commitments, my mother is pro-life and does not support abortion rights. I too am pro-life but I care equally about the lives of the mothers and would not take freedom of choice from any woman.

A favorite pastor, an older man, spoke from the pulpit once of accompanying his son to an open AA meeting and the impact of the staggering honesty he experienced in the room. What struck me about his comment was his surprise that this kind of truth telling existed in the world. Surely if it lives anywhere it should live in the church. I long for us all to put away the cup polishing in support of transparency, knowing that none of us has a righteous leg to stand on.

We define the dark matter in our lives differently—things that cause one persons cheeks to burn I would probably brag about. But one thing is sure—when we move towards our soft vulnerable belly and say something as true as possible we offer the listener or listeners clarity and a chance to breathe, to perhaps hold their own secrets up to the light and then, to tell it like it is.

WE ARE SOBER

The slogan "One day at a time" is central to AA philosophy and contains a message that is twofold. First, we confine our abstinence commitment to the twenty-four hours ahead—and sometimes that particular stretch feels twenty-three hours and thirty minutes too long. The second idea is that we are all on equal sober ground: the newcomer with two days strung together and the old timer with many years under his or her belt, each of us is granted the same daily reprieve.

Most of us in AA know that length of sober time is no guarantee against future drunkenness; it is the work of recovery found in the twelve steps that secures our footing in the present and makes way for a drink free tomorrow that will actually come. Because of this, we're advised not to brag or really even mention how much time we have in the program beyond accepting an annual medallion with the number of years engraved in the center. But, of course, those of us with a lot of time find a way to drop those numbers and look more or less self-effacing as we do it.

Except Burney. She has paid so little attention to her sobriety date that she confuses it with when she started selling a high end line of clothing called Doncaster. Suffice it to say she's strung together enough 24 hours to call it a pilgrimage.

Burney attends an AA meeting every day but Sunday and is easily the best dressed person in the room, though the meetings often start at 6:30 am. She says she was first introduced to alcohol as a sophomore in college when her sister Betsy took her to an off limits roadhouse for chili—and beer. She doesn't remember if the chili was any good but retains a perfect image of her single beer:

"Oh I loved it and the giddy, everybody thinks I'm adorable feeling it gave me"

Alcoholism develops differently among people. Some drink with impunity for many years before a crisis or some internal tipping point removes the ability to control it. Others take a first sip, then another—and are all in. That's me. I felt so completely lacking, so wrong in my skin and about my skin until someone handed me my first beer. Initially I hated the taste but oh Lord I loved the medicine. Suddenly that skin that I'd looked upon as a hide—and a hideous one at that—felt like velvet.

Burney found the velvet too—feeling the soft fuzzy warmth that rose up from her toes and made her cheeks pink. The first drink is sublime—all the others are efforts to keep that slippery vapor from exiting through our pores taking the adorable and leaving the pitiful.

I don't know when my mother completed her mostly well-mannered decent into dependence but I do know when she first sobered up. Burney booked a bed in the same hospital I had recently departed after a 28 day stint for my own alcohol and drug addiction. This was 1985. I managed to stay sober for seven years, after which I tallied up my progress in therapy and spiritual growth, declared myself 'well' and ready to re-enter society as a moderate social drinker. Six years later, thoroughly beaten in my head and heart, I returned to the rooms, ready to follow the program as written.

Burney had her own relapse in Spain after three and a half years of sobriety. She was there with my brother Paul and visited her cousin Graham in a villa on the Mediterranean. Graham and his wife Grace observed the evening cocktail hour ritual and he commented to my mother as she demurred: "Oh Burney, one little ole glass of wine won't hurt you."

Most alcoholics are familiar with the geographical cure, the notion that another place will fix everything that's wrong both internally and externally. There's also the geographical comma, the idea that somehow a lapse or relapse in a location we don't actually live in doesn't count. Burney accepted the glass and confined herself to one drink in Spain but the obsession booked a first class ticket back to the US and was waiting for her when she got home. My mother neglected to mention the incident to my stepfather though he soon noticed the ubiquitous wine glass perched by the kitchen sink and Burney's sudden interest in lunch dates with old friends.

My mother could sidestep her husbands alarm without much trouble but the leaden sense of despair that gripped her in the hours between the last pour of one day and the first pour of the next wasn't so easy to dismiss.

Finally, after a year of mounting misery, she swallowed her pride, picked up a silver chip that indicates the desire for a new way of life and reintroduced herself like a newcomer at an AA meeting. Why is it we feel such shame when we relapse? We alcoholics surely know by now that what comes absolutely naturally to us is drinking. It's the contented sober living that is uncommon and miraculous.

Burney recovered her sobriety along with her joy and hasn't looked back. I asked her why she still makes a meeting nearly every day. She says she never wants to trip over the thought that maybe she's cured; she knows she's vulnerable. But it's more than that. It's more than a clear conscience, better health and freedom from obsession—though it is all those things. These are our people, though many of them come from other paths: high, low and no paths, paths that swing wide of our own and paths that lead next door. Here we speak a common tongue, we nod in complete understanding when someone tells of climbing into a dumpster to retrieve a half empty bottle they threw out declaring: "never again". We hear crazy talk and recognize it as our own. We hear the pain of irreplaceable loss and consequence and feel it. We hear the hope of stringing together a day, a month, a year and share it. It is the language of our affliction.

Burney says: "How many places can you go where you can be totally honest and not condemned for it?" But she was not able to avoid that condemnation with me. My drinking took a toll on everyone in a way that my parent's drinking did not. Somehow they were able to keep the chaos mostly confined to their own souls. They held down jobs and held on to witty repartee, rarely skipping a beat, let alone slurring their words. I have to say I was surprised when Burney told me she was booking a bed in the treatment wing of Petaluma Valley Hospital. I couldn't remember seeing her drunk more than once or twice.

I, conversely, swung from the trees. There was nothing I didn't try, no lengths I wouldn't go and no depths too low. I preferred impolite society, musicians and people on the edge, like me. Burney used threat verses from scripture to try and scare me out of it, tears and disappointment to try and guilt me out of it, Joe grounded me for weeks on end to try and bore me out of it, my father simply stopped speaking to me for days and weeks depending on the offense to try and shame me out of it. Predictably all of it fell on deaf ears while adding to the self-loathing that was my constant companion.

Finally though, it was as simple as asking God for the will to recover. I say simple—a word that, in this case should not be confused with easy. But one day, one ordinary day I walked into an AA meeting and a revolution in my soul began. One ordinary day Burney did the same. It takes one to know one and she has expanded her reservoir of compassion for the loss of reason and choice that accompanies addiction.

At a reunion in South Carolina for my mothers extended family, there was a wall of pictures and newspaper articles honoring my great grand-mother Bessie but hardly a mention beyond one dour photograph of my great grandfather Edward. Burney said that was probably because Edward was an alcoholic—the tree swinger type, like me—who never recovered and finished his long destructive tear through life in a back bedroom shout-ing obscenities at everyone and no one.

Though I'm hard pressed to think of a family that has not been affected by alcohol or drugs, the stigma remains, the idea that at its heart it is a moral failure and can be addressed much like boot-straps. Alcoholism is the fatal disease that insists it doesn't exist—at least not in the mind of the alcoholic. It's the voice in my head that never shuts up as long as it has an audience: "Oh Ashley, one little ole glass of wine won't hurt you." But it did hurt me, over and over again. It hurt my entire family from Edward to my aunt

Betsy to my father who eventually stopped drinking but never recovered and wallpapered the space reserved for vodka with defeat and morose withdrawal. It hurt Burney too and continues with our current generations.

I don't remember the last time I thought about a drink, though I still subscribe to the daily reprieve—I know that voice could start up again when I least expect it. I know too that I'm not cured—I don't have to take the 'you might have a drinking problem' test to know that all my answers are still 'yes' or 'hell yes'.

Contemplating God, who lives outside of time, with whom one day is as a thousand years and a thousand years as a day, I look back on the day I walked into AA. I do not think that a thousand years could contain the gifts of recovery that began that day. Near the top of the pile is the understanding between me and Burney: we are sober, it is a miracle, live it out and pass it on.

BODY

The seven arts of the soul, the shapes that are ours, 26 bones, flat on the floor. Was there anything you enjoyed about the play Mrs. Lincoln? Loss, gain, walk, glide, pivot, separate, assimilate and who's your tailor?

BEAUTY IS ONLY A LIGHT SWITCH

Songwriter Karen Staley, once took bathroom stall graffiti to the bank. She read: "Beauty is only a light switch away" on the stall door in a local coffee shop and repeated the phrase to her co-writer, Bob Dipiero in a songwriting session later that day. Together they wrote: "Take Me As I Am," which went on to be a hit for Faith Hill who ironically, as Karen says, looks good in any light.

My mother would tell you that unlike Faith, she is not a natural beauty but employs an arsenal of technique designed to trick the eyes of the beholder and keep them fixed on her best features. She developed these skills over decades beginning in the late 1950s and early 1960s when she taught a form of charm school called Seven Arts at Riches Department store in Knoxville, Tennessee.

In Seven Arts, style and form were carefully defined and cultivated: this is how one enters a room with grace and confidence, this is how to wear your clothing—rather than letting it wear you, this is how to redirect the eyes, this is loveliness, this is not.

Personally, I love a little make-up—and though I don't think I brushed my hair in the 90s, l have taken to curling irons and hair dryers in the 21st century. I like enhancements and wearing clothes that feel flattering and fit me well. But as my daughter Lily pointed out, the question is, are you expressing yourself or hiding behind a manufactured, idealized representative?

We have made some progress in this culture expanding the notion of what comprises beauty but the current standards continue to occupy a fairly narrow trench—and I rarely meet a woman who doesn't harbor shame over some aspect of her body. I imagine this is true for men too—they are just less likely to say so.

Burney has lived her Seven Arts philosophy through multiple generations and owns it fully so I must say it surprised me to learn that her most significant beauty lesson was at Cedar Crest camp when she was an adolescent.

Camp culture has a hierarchy all its own—often revolving around cabin assignments. In her second year at Cedar Crest, Burney arrived to find her trunk and bunk in the pretentiously named Captain's Cabin along with the equally pretentious popular girls. Who cared if it was all pretentious? My mother was elated, she'd stepped across the threshold of a preferential world previously glimpsed only from a distance.

But on the second day of camp the director paid a visit to Burney and wasted no time on pleasantries saying: "We want you to move to another cabin. There are several girls having difficulty adjusting and we think you would be a help to the counselor." One of the hymns Burney knew by heart began playing in her mind: "I'll go where You want me to go dear Lord, o'er mountain or plain or sea. I'll do what You want me to do dear Lord, I'll be what You want me to be." Her tongue twisted as she responded: "I'll be glad to go." 'Liar,' she thought to herself.

Mountains, plains and seas were one thing, a dusty path to the loser cabin was something else. Burney anticipated bed wetters, cry babies and God only knew what. And speaking of God—how could He? He'd been privy to every prayer of longing to be included, to every slight, to all the leaving out and passing over. She was incensed and did not want to go, do or be anything other than popular.

Grudgingly she packed her trunk and went. The cabin counselor met her at the door and seeing her for the first time, Burney thought: 'Oh this is too much.' One side of the girl's forehead was caved in and made her difficult to look at. She responded to my mother's stare with the explanation that she'd had something called an aneurism when she was younger and now there was steel plate in her head.

Looking back, my mother says she has forgotten the names of all the popular girls at Cedar Crest but she will never forget her counselor Meriel Derby who may have had steel in her head but whose heart was so big, so wide, warm and embracing that within days Burney was on her knees thanking God for putting her in the loser cabin. She told me she loved nothing more than just to be in Meriel's company. When I asked what it was about her, she said Meriel was the most non-judgmental accepting person she'd ever met and that made her utterly beautiful. "She never tried to correct any of the problems belonging to the problem kids, she simply received each cabin mate, including me, for who we were and what we had to contribute, which was often precious little."

I suspect my mother offered more than she gave herself credit for and that the camp director had already seen her capacity to look beyond the superficial into the soul when he asked her to move. Burney may be qualified to teach the Seven Arts but at Cedar Crest she discovered that the rarest and most precious beauty is shaped by kindness and gentleness. It cannot be taught in charm school and it is often mined in the loneliest shafts of suffering.

Nearly every picture of Jesus I've ever seen presents him as winsome and handsome. I wonder. The prophet Isaiah describes him like this: "He has no form or comeliness; And when we see him there is no beauty that we should desire him."(ch 53:2.NKJ) "He is despised and rejected by men, a man of sorrows, acquainted with grief. And we hid, as it were our faces from him ("53:3 NKJ). Maybe Jesus was hard to look at too.

I had a few years myself where no one was saying, 'here's looking at you kid', I was carrying an extra 35 pounds, I was covered in acne and my anger and loneliness brought out every scowling trait. But my disfigurement was born of shame. I never heard the story of Meriel—though I surely

91

could have used it, being a perennial candidate for the loser cabin. Instead, I heard about diets, including on a visit to a pediatrician who gave me my first taste of amphetamines with diet pills. I heard fashion tips and bra interventions using the image of Grandmother Cleveland, whose breasts swung dangerously close to her navel, as a deterrent. I heard the ifs and buts in both my parents appraisals of me, often without a word. And I turned right around and passed those wallpaper ideals on to my kids.

'Beauty is on the inside' is certainly a worn out trope—probably because it's true. Burney taught the Seven Arts: gracious physical comportment, personality development, basic rules for a pleasant speaking voice, hair, make-up, wardrobe and figure control to full classes of attentive women. But I wonder if the sly cat on the cover of the Seven Arts brochure knew that without the animation of hospitality and generosity these skills amounted to little more than empty silhouettes like the god Narcissus gazing with unfulfilled longing at his reflection in the pool until he dies. On the other end of the spectrum is this young woman, Meriel, also gazing—from a profoundly disfigured face, who sees and accepts herself, lifts her eyes to the source of all true loveliness, takes courage and lives.

GOD GIVEN GEOMETRY

My mother has a head for figures but only when they are clothed. Numbers pile up in the corners of her mind, jumbled and confused. In high school Burney had a teacher named Henrietta Weigel for geometry. Miss Weigel had her older sister Betsy a year or two previously and favored her as the front runner of the Parrott clan. Shortly into the school year Miss Weigal made it clear she had written Burney off as hopeless, not only in geometry but in general. My mother struggled through the class willing herself to become small, hoping to escape notice. But vulnerability has a scent and she learned that her teacher had used her as an example one day when addressing another class. Miss Weigel told them, "I feel sorry for the Parrott family; they have one daughter that is very smart but the other daughter is stupid and that must be very difficult for their mother."

In fourth grade I had a teacher, Mr. Yuen who took an instant dislike to me and one day used me as an example of ingratitude and waste. Burney was quick to adopt the California trend toward healthy eating that had not yet trickled down to the elementary school. While other kids found bologna on Wonder Bread with the crusts removed, chips and cookies in their lunch bags, mine had a sandwich made with natural peanut butter or tuna fish on whole wheat bread, carrot sticks and a piece of fruit. I knew I didn't have a single thing anyone would trade with me for. So unless I was starving, I threw the sack away and skipped lunch altogether.

Mr Yuen caught me one day and called me to the front of the class. He retrieved my lunch bag from the garbage and emptied it on his desk, holding up each wadded up, sorry item and pointing out my lack of appreciation for a meal and the hands that provided it. I glanced briefly at my classmates and read the obvious—they wouldn't have eaten those things either. But the disgust they felt for the food transferred easily to me and added to the isolation and loneliness I felt as an East Tennessee transplant in a Marin County school.

Burney managed to survive Miss Weigal and her contempt but not unscathed. Years later she was performing with a Junior League choir at an event and spotted Miss Weigal in the audience. Burney froze and was unable to sing a note as melody became geometry and flew from her heart to the pit of her stomach.

I asked what she did and she said, "Well, it was a turning point. I thought to myself, why have I allowed this woman who means nothing to me so much power in my life?" She thought of the 6th verse of the 18th Psalm: "In my anguish I cried out to The Lord, and He answered by setting me free. The Lord is with me; I will not be afraid. What can man do to me?" (NIV).

Later in that same Psalm David writes, "He brought me out into a spacious place. He delivered me because He delighted in me." (vs19 NIV/NKJ). Burney stepped into that spacious place, found her voice midway through the song and silently sent Miss Weigal packing.

In truth, men, women and children can do a lot to us. We routinely hurt one another in word and deed. I don't know if Burney put her shame entirely to rest that day, I do know that retiring my own shame and stepping into self-acceptance is a lifelong work involving grief and a daily intention. I have no acumen for the points, lines, angles, surfaces and solids of geometry either, my love is for the curve of the word, written, spoken and sung. To my knowledge I've never been publicly declared stupid but I have been declared undesirable. And, in an ironic twist, my mother has certainly contributed to my sense of inadequacy. I know now it was unintentional on her part and certainly not deliberately cruel. She would say: "I just wanted you to be your best self." But, according to whom?

Perhaps Burney hasn't entirely stilled Miss Weigal's voice; perhaps there is lingering detritus. Because at the bottom of her criticisms is a strong desire to protect her children from a scornful world. My parents both subscribed to the idea that looking good was, is and always will be the best revenge and in this culture of such absurd unattainable beauty standards that require procedures to reach, who can argue?

My determination to separate from my well-appointed parents and cultivate my own style—stylish, or not—was nothing short of a subversive battle cry. I could feel the disappointment when I emerged in my hippie head bands and baggy jeans. They both chorused to me more than once, individually and in unison: "You could be so attractive....if......" If I lost weight, if I changed my hair—or even bothered to brush it, if I wore tailored clothes in the right colors, if I learned how to apply make-up.

The message was the same—you're not quite—almost but not quite. In her book "Women Who Run With The Wolves" Clarissa Pinkola Estes asks the crucial question: "So why do women keep trying to bend and fold themselves into shapes that are not theirs?" The answer lies of course in those two little words: 'not quite'.

I too have communicated disappointment to my children in the area of appearance. I'm heartsick about this but it's true. I too was motivated by a desire to protect them, a desire for them to feature their best features in order to gain love and admiration. I too wanted them to reflect well on me and have just begun to dismantle these notions and seek their forgiveness. I have forgiven my parents and am working on forgiving myself—the hardest task of all. I too cherish the 18th Psalm but honestly, I don't know that I'll ever be entirely free where body image is concerned. I feel anxiety when I miss a day of exercise and I look upon women who have embraced fat culture with a mixture of awe, admiration and horror. The most honest thing I can say about my body is, I have reached an uneasy truce with it. I turn to Macrina Wiederkehrs prayer: "Oh God help me to believe the truth about myself, no matter how beautiful it is" and say it often.

Rev Becca Stevens says that love without judgment is the most radical love of all. And nowhere is it more radical or revolutionary or heaven sent, than when turned homeward to ourselves.

THE ACTION ON THE GROUND

In college I spent very little of my time in class and a lot of time in local clubs playing music and drinking. My friend Pam Tillis and I had a folk duo and in those days, there was no shortage of venues on the Cumberland Avenue strip that skirts the University of Tennessee campus. I got to know some of the other regular performers around the clubs, including Bill who operated as a one man band. He played a bass drum with one foot and a souped up keyboard contraption with the other. He played guitar and harmonica and sang too but the action was on the ground. His feet were in constant motion, moving independently and even out of synch with one another. One night we had a conversation at the bar where he began to gush about feet in general:

"Amazing instruments" he said, "Hundreds of tiny bones exquisitely fit together—incredible what they can do. I mean, 25 per cent of the bones in your body are in your feet! I love em. I really love em and I love to make love to them. Has anyone ever made love to your feet?" he asked. "Um no", I said, scooting my bar stool away. "Don't knock it til you've tried it." he said, winking. At that time in my life I had plenty of game for just about anything anyone suggested but here I drew a disgusted line and made it a point to avoid Bill.

One look at my mother's feet though and Bill would have been in a fetish frenzy. They're not small, size 9s I think, but they are symmetrically perfect, feminine and strong, neither wide or narrow, just shapely. Maybe I've given this kind of consideration to Burney's feet because up until recently I looked upon mine as similar to sausages overstuffing their casings. I have extra large hands and feet and I've not always felt particularly friendly towards them. But time and experience have eased the self consciousness and demonstrated all the remarkable things these big hands and feet can do. I think of Michael Phelps, his double joints, merman build and of course his flipper feet, all of which set him apart in an extraordinary way.

My sister Jennie distributes essential oils and counts me among her customers. The accompanying handbook has a large diagram of a foot and though I know very little about reflexology I have long been aware that the foot is in many ways, the body's control panel. Who knew you could access your brain through your big toe or your liver via your instep? I have an oil that I apply below my second toe for any respiratory issues, I have another one that I put on the soles of my feet to beef up my immune system and so it goes—there is a corresponding spot on the foot chart for every system, organ and gland in the body.

In my youth and misadventure my feet kept me running away from the things I was afraid of and straight into trouble. In age and recovery I have been running towards things—like good health. This morning I ran a few miles around Santa Rosa Beach, Florida, filling my lungs with salty air and gazing out over the Emerald Coast. My feet have carried me into love and marriage, family and friendships, onstage and off, uphill and down. Mostly, they have held me up and kept me moving. I've even learned to plant them and be still.

My mother is still moving too, though not at all like she wants to. These days she has put her sexy footwear on the shelf in favor of low heels and arch support. She hasn't succumbed to Birkenstocks though I tell her there are great new designs. Burney insists they still look like tractor tire remnants held together with leashes. At a recent family event I smiled when she walked in wearing a pair of blingy sandals looking kind of kittenish. So much has been taken from her, driving her to the sensible aisle. But even as all these good things come to an end, it's nice to catch a breeze from another decade once in a while.

THE METHUSELAH GENE

When I asked Burney about the advantages of old age, she guffawed and said, "That's like saying: Was there anything you particularly enjoyed about the play Mrs Lincoln?" "Mom", I start and she interrupts me laughing—"Don't get me wrong, I love shriveled skin, yellow teeth, varicose veins, stiff legs—do I need to go on?"

I tell her the question is actually serious but she needs a moment to recover from her litany of ills before she can answer. She comforts herself saying, compared to Methuselah she's still in her infancy. Methuselah—the old man of record in the bible was 969 when he finally gave up the ghost. My great grandmother, Bessie was three weeks shy of 101 when she passed. The family attributed her many years to a gracious temperament and clean living but that doesn't explain my great grandfather, Edward. He racked up 97 hard scrabble years before his departure with a nasty personality, a lot of booze, pipe tobacco, meals held together with lard and coffee you could stand a spoon in.

I used to appreciate the long roots of our family tree. Now I fear them slightly—probably because I have a sinking suspicion my mind will vacate long before I do. I try to keep myself afloat with body and mind pursuits that range from memorizing scripture and poetry to crossword puzzles to

101

french to meditation to exercise every day. But in the dust to dust march, gravity wins—always.

In bad weather I sometimes run at a YMCA that caters to seniors. Those seniors have fully embraced their special status and use it as license to act up. The gym has a generous track with three lanes and a large posted sign giving walkers the two inside lanes and runners the remaining one on the outside. But I can plan on an unpleasant encounter nearly every time I go to run. Sometimes it's because of 3 white headed ladies strolling together side by side (I've even seen them arm in arm) choking up the lanes. Most of the time it's a lone person, shuffling along in the running lane or just standing in it to passively (aggressively) gaze out the nearest window. It's maddening. I practice holding my tongue but once when I couldn't get around the three women taking their YMCA 'togetherhood' tee shirts entirely too seriously, I stopped running and said to them in what I'm pretty sure was my indoor voice: "Good morning ladies, can you please stick to the walking lanes and leave the running lane open?"

All three of them whirled around gasping and shrank back from me as if I was an ogress in lululemon barreling into their peaceful morning. They complied—grudgingly but I would not be surprised if a complaint card detailing my brief reign of terror on the upstairs track landed in the suggestion box that day.

Burney gives me a little insight into this senior entitlement. One of the first advantages of old age she manages to come up with when pressed is: "I get away with stuff" To my mind, she has been getting away with 'stuff' all her life but I think the difference is she no longer feels the need to even pretend to follow the rules—unless she wants to. She uses her age and humor to deflect any unpleasantness.

When I finally get her to focus on the remote possibility of benefits accompanying one's eighties she becomes thoughtful about the distillation of advancing years. She says: "I have fewer responsibilities and a greater awareness of what really matters." I don't have to ask what matters to her, I know she will say God and people. And although she is not as enthusiastic as I am about getting rid of her accumulated belongings, she does recognize that the freedom from all the care and feeding of property leaves space for expanding these crucial relationships.

My sister Jennie, Jennie's husband Jim and especially my brother Paul and my sister in law Jasmine do nearly all the heavy lifting with Burney but the extended friendships she has formed with young women and men make her feel engaged and vital and also offer reassurance that whatever need might arise, it will be swiftly met with many loving hands. I'm thankful for all the care that comes her way and I know too that my exasperation over her political pronouncements, her attachment to things like junk mail and products she uses once and crams into her little linen closet—are no big deal for others. They love her as is. I mostly love her as is.

Of God Burney says, "You know for most of my life my prayers have been directed to the Father but I talk to Jesus throughout the day now and ask for his company. That's new for me—maybe because when I was younger I didn't think I needed him minute to minute but now as my footing becomes less sure, it's a great comfort." "That makes perfect sense," I say, thinking of all Jesus' miracles that had to do with restoring someones footing.

How hard it must be when we begin to stumble from the ground we thought we owned and must face being taken where we don't want to go and stripped of even the smallest decisions. I do not want to be in the state of California when Burney surrenders her car keys but I know there will be drivers lined up for the pleasure of her company.

I turn my thoughts to Dylan Thomas' poem: Do Not Go Gentle Into That Good Night, to the seniors wreaking their brand of havoc at the Bellevue YMCA, to my mother relishing getting away with stuff and simultaneously hoarding it. Next time I see those white heads bobbing in my running lane I'm gonna stand down. I'm gonna cheer them on and urge them to: "Rage, rage against the dying light!", to act up and declare, "We are here! We are here!" because they are and the rest of us are richer for it.

103

LOSS AND GAIN AND A VERY FULL LIFE

One of the advantages of menopause is that it is followed by a rinse cycle of forgetting years. The first time I brought it up with my mother, asking what it was like, she said she didn't remember it. I thought: 'So, it must not be too bad...'. But once I had shed my own fertility skin, I'd answered that question exhaustively for myself. Flooding, flashing, sweating, not sleeping and enduring endless days of menace directed at anyone in my path finally gave way to a relative calm. I revisited the topic recently and got a different answer. Burney said her memories of menopause were primarily emotional. She felt desolate and that her life amounted to little more than failure.

My mother had recently returned to sobriety from a year of relapse and added that going to AA meetings helped ease her bleak frame of mind and refocused her on moving forward. I suspect this is the reason she makes the fellowship such a priority in her life after thirty plus years of sobriety. It continues to refresh and reorient her thinking and attitudes.

In her book "The Wisdom Of Menopause", Christiane Northrup posits the theory that many women find that out of the madness of having their brains catch fire and their hormones plummet into obscurity, an exit ramp appears. In the midst of internal upheaval they realize that all the compensating, putting up and keeping up they've devoted their lives to is no longer acceptable or even possible.

But what begins as an ending can also provide the opportunity for re-ordering and repossessing our lives and selves. For Burney this meant a commitment to sobriety and recovery. For me it also meant simplifying and distilling down to what really mattered: how I spent my time and with whom, putting my creative life front and center rather than behind my list of chores, addressing my people pleasing ways and living truthfully, but also without offense if at all possible. It meant letting go of relationships that were peripheral or had run their course. This is not easy for someone who makes a concerted effort to be all things to all people and just as the symptoms of menopause are not without discomfort and emotional pain, I faced significant struggle in this transition. And then, even in the midst of finding contentment in the stripping and reordering, I too looked upon my life as little more than failure.

Maybe it is simply death of vision, the dreams we carry through the heroic part of our journey that never materialize or, if they do materialize, don't survive, now feel out of reach and the ashes are…..ashes.

Mary Pipher describes the transition into old age as a boundary crossing in her book Women Rowing North. She writes: "….everything interesting happens at borders." I have to agree and I find the most interesting part of this strange new land is I have exchanged my dreams for curiosity. 'What would you have me do?' I pray. 'What do you want?' I hear. I think the answer is, though I still very much want to matter, I want to matter less and offer more.

This complex crossing from loss to gain to loss again has a story for each of us. There is the chance of new spontaneity with sex. Burney says, "I didn't suddenly become crazed with lust or anything like that but I was gratified to….." I interrupt her, "Mom, let's stop at gratified." There is freedom to explore. I went to Paris for 3 weeks alone to study French and learn the city one 'rue' at a time. It was my ticket to the world, the recognition I can go anywhere with a little dough and the 'want to'.

I wouldn't trade anything for the years with my children. They shaped me as much as any experience I've had and one day I hope for grandchildren. But their exit offered a new freedom and I'm engrossed with opportunities to learn and create. Burney's initial post-menopausal activities kept her far afield with her own opportunities—and kept me complaining: "So much for the doting grandmother." She's come full circle now, living two doors down from my brother and maintaining an open door policy with his four kids.

As far as evaluating our lives in terms of success or failure, my mothers nearly 88 years are bursting at the seams with love and community. That's not surprising, Burney has cultivated those things from day one. What is surprising and even miraculous is that I could say the same thing about my life. To be seen, known and loved, to find I am capable of love—this is the real measure.

My therapist friend Linda had a client who'd been married 5 or 6 times. She'd been divorced and widowed repeatedly and was now single. Hearing her story for the first time, Linda commented, "That's a lot of loss." The woman gazed at her and said brightly: "Yes—and a lot of gain too." That's the border toll, a lot of loss, a lot of gain and, by the grace of God, a very full life.

A GREAT SET OF GAMS

There are a lot of ways to walk. Burney will tell you she's covered considerable ground wandering, striding, strolling, skipping and lately, staggering through her eighty plus years. My mother has a long history with all things leggy. She was a traveling saleswoman in the early 1960s selling shoe paint and glitter for Shu Mak Up and hypnotizing her customers with words like 'silhouette' and 'ensemble' into an inexplicable willingness to paint and repaint their pumps to match their outfits. Before that she taught young women in a department store charm school to put their show feet forward and pivot for emphasis as they joined the society catwalk.

I ask her if she has any leg stories and get a quick response about a work trip and a stay in a swank hotel. Rather than a baroque mirror or shelves of bottles and highball glasses, the long bar in the cocktail lounge was backed by a thick window that provided a below surface view of the swimming pool, like a human aquarium.

Did my mother know she was the underwater entertainment for afternoon drinkers when she and her friend decided to wind down with a swim? She didn't say but she certainly caught on later when they stopped in the lounge for a drink before dinner. A man at the bar turned and said loudly: "Here comes the girl with the prettiest legs in the swimming pool!"

109

"Were you offended? I ask" "No, he was so lit, he probably couldn't have stood up. I did feel a little bit like a show dog though." Burney likes to be admired, she dresses for compliments and receives them happily. So where is the boundary between compliment and show dog?

My friend Becca tells me that in her 20s, a man whistling at her on the street would prompt a double bird and a righteous "Fuck off!". Now in her 60s, she says an occasional whistle feels pretty good. How well I know. I'm reminded every day of the loss of my vitality, not to mention elasticity when someone calls me 'maam'. It will get worse too. Eventually we'll be reduced to 'hon' or 'dear' and finally, 'young lady,' the signal all is truly lost.

In the face of aging and invisibility, a little objectification seems a welcome distraction. And though I would be first to challenge unwanted attention or predatory behavior (like the guy in the park the other day who tried to start a conversation with me while he was peeing into the woods) or a hotel bar that offers a plate glass peep show into the swimming pool, I'd also be a liar if I said that male admiration didn't feel good—because often it does.

It's an interesting question in a culture that has long used a single sense— the eyes—to evaluate people and establish a standard of beauty. I've done it too—I remember an encounter with a ridiculously handsome guy in my 20's. When we started dating I attached all sorts of inner attributes to his gorgeous frame. But in the end that frame was just a container and he was a dumb ass with nothing to say.

Back to Burney's legs. She said she rarely had inappropriate advances or comments from men—and if she did, she employed her pivot and walked away. That's a reflection of the real beauty of my mother's legs: she has walked into or away from whatever she wanted—with confidence, with faith, with fear, with children in tow, with a clear direction and without. Anyone can be born with shapely limbs—but not everyone can use those limbs to shape their destinies quite so effectively.

I did some walking myself, crossing the country back to Tennessee and eventually Nashville to a career in music. I walked into motherhood, marriage and motherhood again without the slightest qualifications—just a high degree of 'want to'. I walked in and out of recovery until I stayed. Sometimes I lament the loss of my intrepid youth, feeling dangerously close to sensible shoes and rubber soles for my 'walking'. But in this stretch of 'why not?' I continue to walk into things that feel quite beyond me to master and even on a fruitless day, there is a vitality in showing up. Burney maintains her constitutionals at Shollenberger Park, avoiding the sections of uneven ground, her concession to nearing 90, but still in motion.

I noticed a picture in the paper yesterday of a woman training for a marathon with a running blade. She lost part of a leg in an accident and began to regain her life and footing in a running group for people with prosthetics. Thinking of her courage and willingness, thinking that in the end, it's not about the legs, it's about the package that they carry, I thought to myself: 'Now that is a great set of gams'.

LEAVING BURNEY'S LOOK BOOK

My husband, Kenny describes his initial impression of me as: "…dressed like a schoolteacher, singing like Etta James". It took over 40 years and 2300 miles between me and Burney to create a space of confidence where my outsides started to match my insides. Before that, my clothes were fairly conservative while my music (and behavior) was all edge. If it is true that what we wear telegraphs who we are and how we feel about ourselves, at least to some extent, then what I wore basically said: 'I have no idea who I am or where I belong but I definitely do not fit here.' Even now, when I'm in a group of super groomed, super soft women, I want to run as far and as fast as I can.

If I ask my mother what her fashion rules are she'll insist she doesn't have any and then tick them off in order:

1. People should pay realistic attention to cut, fit and color when shopping rather than trends.

2. People should dress to their body types

3. Skirt lengths should be determined by age and the shape of a woman's legs.

Then comes the rant—this one about heavier girls Burney describes as,

"....stuffing their beefy bodies into mini skirts, leggings and boots. Honestly, she says, they look like country hams hanging from hooks." I think to myself, 'I was one of those girls, no wonder I needed to relocate.'

When Burney is exposed to what she views as a particularly unfortunate bit of costuming on anyone, her response often includes: 'poor dear'—as if the woman in question is wandering haplessly through life wearing an outfit she is either unaware of or has been draped in against her will. I wonder if it occurs to my mother that maybe the clothes are intentional, maybe the wearer is an iconoclast and loves different shades of purple and skirts with fringe, maybe they don't care if their butts look big in their boho pants, maybe the 'my little pony' tee shirt transports them to a kinder, gentler era.

Perhaps these things do occur to Burney but not enough to put a damper on her mission to right garment wrongs. She tells me that seeing so many unattractive ensembles supplied the motivation to sell Doncaster, a high end brand sold in seasonal trunk shows by appointment.

Burney went to great lengths to find the right wardrobe pieces for her clients. She said tailoring was the secret and there was no overestimating the value of a good seamstress. She found one two towns over and took care of her customers alterations on her own dime. She gave sample pieces to women who could not afford the retail prices. Confidence through clothing was her war whoop.

So much of what drives us has little to do with the present and everything to do with our own often bitter history. At 13, Burney arrived at a tea dance in Knoxville wearing a full skirted blue taffeta ball gown that her grandmother had painstakingly stitched for her. The other older girls wore short modern dresses and laughed when they saw her calling her and the dress 'freaky'. I imagine Burney drew a line in the sand then and there like Scarlett O'Hara, vowing she would never be freaky again.

My mother has been doling out fashion confidence ever since to women of all shapes and sizes—with the exception of her daughters. All of us had a rite of passage that included taking a stand against her style interventions. I find it ironic and probably inevitable that the 'freakiness' Burney shunned

114

became a part of my wardrobe ambition.

Currently I feel pretty happy and confident about my clothes, mostly because I feel like me when I wear them. I separated but also assimilated. I found a good tailor, dropped my mothers exclamation mark after the word: 'accessorize', gave up coordinates, declaring them little more than adult 'Garanimals' and took a car load of nearly all the Doncaster Burney had gifted me with to Good Will. I kept a beautifully made dark skirt and blouse for funerals and a red coat dress I liked. I wore the coat dress to a funeral too but also over jeans and a tee shirt when I played Saturday Night Live with John Hiatt—an unintended statement that somehow, we carry all things forward in becoming.

As for Burney, she's a long way from the taffeta incident. Someone asked me at an event which one was my mother and I said—she's the old lady over there in the red leather jacket. "Hmmm, who's her tailor?"

CULTURE

Basic rules of civility and decency in company, quite fetching, don't you agree? I'll take truth for a wilted rose, white supremacy, white exceptionalism, white heroism and the color line between us, agents of good, agents of ill, agents of mercy.

WASHINGTONS RULES

George Washington's Basic Rules of Civility And Decent Behavior in Company and Conversation are not Washington's composition, though he adopted them at sixteen when his schoolmaster asked him to copy them by hand for an exercise in penmanship and chivalry. They were created by French Jesuits in 1595 and translated to English initially around 1640.

Burney has observed codes of behavior all her life, some handed down from her parents, particularly her school teacher mother, and some she has picked up in the course of living. She repeats to me a few rules, laughing at the frilly language, but not the sentiment—she abides them all. And few could argue with these mostly gentle admonitions For example:

2 When in company, put not your hands to any part of the body not usually discovered.

#3 Show nothing to your friend that may affright him.

4 In the presence of others, sing not to yourself with a humming noise nor drum with your fingers or feet. (I would personally add, nor shout into your cell phone forcing the community around you to endure your side of a conversation)

53 Run not in the streets, neither go too slowly with your mouth open, go

119

not shaking your arms, kick not the dirt with your feet, go not upon the toes nor in a dancing fashion.

97 Put not another bite into your mouth till the former be swallowed. Let not your morsels be too big for the jowls.

100 Cleanse not your teeth with the tablecloth napkin, fork or knife but if others do it, let it be done without a peep to them.

All 110 rules have in common consideration of those in our immediate vicinity. These days, formal training in deportment has been largely discarded in our culture, maybe because it seems pretentious and fussy in a society that is preoccupied with weightier issues of injustice and unrest. Maybe because it challenges peoples 'rights' and independence. But I, my rebel heart not withstanding, labored to teach my children good manners and a few formal dance steps. I sent them to Cotillion to learn basic ballroom dancing and how to set an elaborate table—things I knew they would never tolerate learning from me. I asked them to respond to their elders with 'yes ma'am and yes sir' and I urged them away from shoe gazing and into direct eye contact and firm—but not painful—handshakes. I did it for two reasons. I wanted them to venture out into the world with a certain level of ease in social interaction and I wanted them to begin to look away from themselves and towards those around them with respect and regard.

All of them openly despised Cotillion and said they were the only kids they knew in Williamson County forced to go to the advanced class. They deliberately mis-set the table for holidays and ate with their mouths open when they knew I was watching. I was always watching. I don't think we finished a single meal without the word 'manners' inserted as an imperative, always by me and typically ignored.

But now that they are out of the house and in the world, they all present well and are confident in most any situation that if they don't know the unwritten rules, they surely know the ones that are posted.

I learned those same rules, my parents saw to it and I have to say, I like knowing and in some cases using them.. I ask Burney her essential etiquette and she says: The Golden Rule, overlooking the lapses of others and not singling out their transgressions as being more despicable than her own. Gratitude is on her list alongside authenticity because she despises fawning and excessive cheer but is ever on the lookout for ways to be appreciative without being phony. More than anything she says, she wants to be aware of the other person, to help them feel at ease, especially in an unfamiliar setting.

Burney says she has unwittingly caused offense because of her own ignorance and self-involvement, and remembers an interaction with her landlady Mrs Wales when she was living in Scotland. They were having a discussion about the differences between Americans and Brits and my mother expressed surprise at the infrequency of British bathing. She said, "Americans are always bathing, it's a national pastime." Mrs Wales and her daughter, Mary exchanged glances but said nothing.

In a moment of clarity my mother realized the reason they were not bathing was because of her own daily lengthy showers and the shortage of hot water. World War two had plunged many parts of the British empire into severe deprivation and Mrs Wales had given what little hot water she was allowed to my mother. On another occasion Burney saw Mrs Wales washing a wool suit by hand in a bucket of water and said, "Mrs Wales, why don't you have that dry-cleaned so it doesn't lose its shape?" Mrs Wales said, "Oh we haven't had a dry cleaner in Edinburgh for some time now, the chemicals were needed for the war effort." My mother loved Mrs Wales and would not have knowingly offended her for anything but she learned another valuable lesson in etiquette: think before you speak—particularly on foreign soil.

Years later my parents were taking an extended trip in Europe and met up with Mrs Wales and Mary to drive through the English countryside on a pub crawl. They stopped for lunch at a cafe and as they were leaving Mrs Wales excused herself for the loo. She returned, some time later wearing a turban she had fashioned from the toilet paper. My mother carefully inquired about her creation and Mrs. Wales said, "Oh my dear it was just so soft and appealing and I have never seen such a gorgeous shade of pink, far too pretty to be hidden in a stall. It's quite fetching don't you agree?" Burney said she did agree and Mrs. Wales settled happily in the back seat of the car, a vision with her crown. My father did not agree and whispered tersely to my mother that he would not be seen in a pub or anywhere else with a woman wearing a toilet paper hat.

Burney saw it differently though. She remembered her hard won understanding of the loss of luxuries great and small during the war and she suspected the regulation tissue currently widely available to the middle class was very likely as rough and coarse as a corn cob. Mrs Wales was obviously surprised and delighted to find this small extravagance in a ladies room of all places and she wanted to take a few yards of it with her when she left. Burney deftly turned to Mrs Wales as they parked the car in the next village and suggested that she might want to leave her enchanting creation in the car, to keep it from being crushed. Mrs. Wales agreed and my father breathed a sigh of relief.

In his biography on President Washington, Mason Locke Weems, generally known as Parson Weems, wrote: "….it was no wonder every body honoured him who honoured every body. Not only did Washington practice the rules of civility with companions, but

he observed them with the entire nation." The whole list can be distilled down to the first rule:

#1 Every Action done in Company, ought to be with Some Sign of Respect, to those that are Present.

And also the last one:

#110 Labor to keep alive in your breast that little spark of celestial fire called conscience.

And yet.

Washington was a slaveholder and though he eventually came to oppose slavery, he did not abolish it, nor did he free his slaves until his death.

We love our heaps of stone. Thirty-three U.S. states have statues in tribute to Washington. In the District of Columbia, in addition to the Washington monument, there are busts, sculptures, seals and stained glass in memorial throughout the city. For some,

monuments represent our glorious history and heritage as a nation. But for others, many of them serve as reminders of oppression and suffering—and inequality. Knowing of his reputation as a humble and just man, I wonder what Washington himself would have said about having his statue toppled and graffiti sprayed in Oregon. He might have taken offense, but he might just as easily have heard the sound of Americans with a scant serving of the democratic citizenry he labored nearly all his life to establish, voicing their pain and rage.

Now, our nation is in a sea change with the onset of Coronavirus and a curtain torn and ragged with repeated exposure of the ongoing racial injustice that plagues us. Many of us have lost much in the midst of this quarantine but perhaps we can begin to find our collective soul. I don't believe unity is always founded in agreement—though it's nice when it is. But the stronger more resilient unity is often forged in disagreement and a willingness to let go of our own cherished notions for the sake of the whole. I'm not suggesting tearing down every statue and monument but I am suggesting earnest, open conversations and the effort to hear the perspectives and experience of others along with considering relocating or doing away entirely with some of the more controversial memorials—and replacing them with something more truthful and inclusive.

Thinking about the last rule of civility, I have to say I don't look upon the tiny spark of celestial fire in me as conscience, I look upon it as the presence of Jesus. Jesus—who set aside his crown and took a posture that was meek and lowly. It is this presence, this indirect light in me that makes it possible to listen and love—even and especially when it is costly. Lifting our heroes to unnatural heights—which frankly, is anything above ground level, could very well keep us from ever seeing eye to eye.

WHAT WAS THE QUESTION?

Burney sold Doncaster clothes in trunk shows for years, mining the top of the sales chart and routinely winning bonuses and trips. For a while she had a district manager she didn't get along with, claiming the woman was a poor leader who did not delegate well or guide the sales team efficiently.

Perhaps sensing my mother's frustration, the manager asked her at one point: "Do you like the way I manage the district?" Burney said cautiously, "I'm not sure I understand the things you do." "Well, the other woman responded, do you like the way I manage you?" Long pause. "No."

My mother told her: "I have good experience in fashion retail but this is a new way of selling and I'm often exhausted trying to figure it out. I feel you've asked me to do additional things that were not my responsibility and when I did them I never got any recognition or compensation." I don't know how the conversation ended but I imagine the last word was a chilly one.

Later that year, at the annual banquet honoring the top tier of the sales force, Burney perched on her chair at her assigned table, confident that her numbers were high on the board, ready to spring at the sound of her name and claim her prize. Her manager stood and called forward the outstanding women in her district, handing them sterling silver cream pitchers and personal accolades. When Burney's turn came, she was silently given a single, wilted rose.

I think maybe my mother misunderstood her boss's question

When someone tells me they want to know what I really think I'm reminded of a friend who gave me mixes of his CD to listen to once asking for an honest response to the songs and the recording. I told him. I told him the things I thought were great, then I told him where I felt the weaknesses were. He hardly spoke to me again and I know I too, misunderstood the question. He was not asking me to critique his work, he was asking me if he still mattered, if he had something of value to bring to the table. He was asking me to be in his corner and to care enough to listen to his hard work. These days, when someone asks me what I honestly think, I keep that in mind, that maybe what they are really saying is—what do you like or love about me? What is my value?

I asked Burney if she'd adjusted her devotion to honesty in light of the bedraggled rose incident and though she agreed that it is not always wise to tell the truth to those in authority over you, anything less would be anathema to her. And yet, if we are listening carefully then we take in not only what is said but sometimes more importantly, what isn't. I think Burney misunderstood my unasked question all those years she was offering me grooming critiques. What I wanted to know, what I still want to know is can I be loved? As is?

I wonder what would have happened if my mother had confined her response to her struggle with trying to adapt to a new selling practice and then asked for help. I bet she would have gotten that cream pitcher.

Burney probably felt she needed to let her boss know how her methods were impacting the team—and maybe she did. There's certainly a place for criticism and in a society where truth is relative to the point of irrelevance, a well placed word or sentence can be a gift to someone—whether they take it or not.

These days when I'm contemplating a potentially thorny exchange, I start with the obvious: does this need to be said? If it does, how? I know I'm not always going to get it right—sometimes I get what I need in the messiness of it, like when I pick a fight with Kenny over something trivial because I feel invisible and want him to see me.

Burney said once in Saks she bumped into an older woman and was in the middle of apologizing profusely for not paying attention when she realized she was talking to a mannequin. My mother laughed and said, "Oh how silly of me, I thought you were real."

That's the quest as we go through life bumping into each other—to be real and to hope for real in return.

OTHER MOTHERS

I understood very little of the suffering in the black community when I was a child. My parents divorce brought a succession of African American women into our home and our lives as maids and caregivers, all of whom contributed to my security and wellbeing, but by then I'd already fallen in love with the handsome woman that worked for my grandparents.

Eva was soft spoken, hard working and anxious to please. Her husband George did the yard work and smoked cigarettes on the stoop, muttering about: "…them snakes in the bushes". My mother traveled for her job and occasionally my sister and I went home with Eva on the weekends. I liked how the kids in her neighborhood would crowd around us and pet us like we were exotic animals. We played games with them in the streets until dark and slept in a giant four poster in the front bedroom. Going to Eva's house meant special attention and in those days, most of the special attention I was getting at home involved a spanking for bad behavior.

In adolescence my father employed a woman named Betty Rose to keep house and in the summers he hired Eva's nieces Sevaria and Brenda to keep an eye on us during our visits while he worked. The sisters played R&B records and tried in vain to teach me dance steps. Betty was the pianist and choir director at her church and taught me gospel songs. I recognize that my experience of black culture would never have happened in a social setting. I am a product of the segregated south. The people that expanded and enriched my life and identity were subjected to cruelty and confinement that threatened their own lives and identities. But in our family, we looked upon ourselves as the good guys.

My grandmother employed a woman named Rosa Belle in my mother's childhood. Burney said Rosa Belle was stern and no nonsense. "I dreaded having my hair washed, she did not spare me or my tangles. When I cried out she would declare: I don't have time to comb each hair. You're gonna have to stand the pain."

Rosa Belle may not have had much of a bedside manner but she had plenty of street smarts and during the depression when men came to the door looking for a meal or a hand out she would size them up and decide who got fed and who was sent packing. Burney asked her why she turned some men away and she said, "I look em in the eye and then I know if they are no good."

My grandfather suffered his own financial losses in those days and both my mother and Rosa Belle overheard him weeping once to my grandmother saying he didn't know how they were going to make it. No one in the family had ever seen Papa cry like that and it devastated my mother. Rosa Belle, however, was prompted to immediate action. She barged into my grandparents conversation and said, "How much do you need?"

Papa told her and she reached under her uniform and took out a large wad of bills secured in the elastic that held up her stockings. My shocked grandparents asked her where she got all that cash. Rosa Belle told them she was the treasurer of the Mt. Olive Baptist Church and in charge of the offering. Papa said, "Rosa Belle, you can't loan me that money, it's a sacred charge." Rosa Belle said, "Mr Paul I trust you with my life."

Papa replied: "And I trust you with mine". He borrowed the money and paid it back forging another link in their lifelong bond of friendship and mutual admiration.

After the death of my mother's baby brother Michael, Rosa Belle was

130

stricken with chronic lumbago and torn with grief over the loss of a child she had loved as her own. The doctor suggested a change in climate might help and she moved to New York where she had family. Rosa Belle went to work for a toy manufacturer, working the assembly line. She had plenty of time to think on that line and she remembered how Michael used to 'help' his daddy fish. The rod was too long for him to hold by himself but he loved turning the reel. Rosa Belle went to her bosses and suggested they make a child sized authentic fishing pole. They took her advice and it became their most popular toy. Rosa Belle was promptly taken off the assembly line and promoted to factory forewoman. My grandfather kept up with her and took her to dinner every time his travels took him to New York. Remembering Rosa Belle and her father, Burney said, "When she got that promotion, daddy was as proud as he would have been with one of his own children." In many ways, the people of color in our lives were viewed as children, needing our guidance and protection rather than as equals, needing our respect and recognition. I did not know the terms 'white exceptionalism', 'white supremacy' or 'white heroism' but we lived it out, no question—though I don't think Burney would see it that way.

Following World War II in an interview with a French journalist, the author Richard Wright responded to a question about the 'negro' problem in America with the now famous quote: "There is no negro problem in the United States, there is only a white problem." Perhaps it is less an issue of race and more an issue of humanity, of fear and hatred of those that are different from us, of the need to feel superior to someone else in order to matter.

I don't know that I would have felt the weight of my own responsibility if I had not had the benefit of these other mothers who loved me so well. But even though I viewed them as members of my family, I did not understand the color line W.E. Dubois wrote about until I saw the anger and grief in Eva's eyes when we invited her to my sister's engagement party. She told my father that she would only come in a uniform and work in the kitchen, which she did.

I used to spend time with my friend Pastor Hart in Nashville's inner city, thinking maybe I could do some good. Pastor quickly disavowed me of that notion of heroic white 'drive-by' and then demonstrated what she could do and was doing with her simple immediate way of acceptance and encouragement of people. She fed them, she hugged them, she welcomed them, she adopted them. Often she put her roof over their heads. She was for many members of her community, their other mother and gave them the gift of love and presence. When I came by her place on Jefferson Street asking what I could do, she would tell me to: "make em a sandwich and give em a hug."

In these days of vast racial divides, of profiling, police brutality, gutted black neighborhoods and generations lost to violence, a hug seems absurdly simplistic. But Pastor knew that if we don't look each other in the eye and treat each other with humanity and dignity, if we don't learn that there is a need not only to step up but also step back to make room for the other person to step forward, if we don't recognize that equality is the strength of our nation, not to mention one of the hallmarks of the Gospel, then the fault line between us and them at the bottom of all these ills will continue to expand and destabilize us. And the shifting ground is no respecter of persons. When we fall, we all fall.

SPIN

When my kids were in grade school any news of a classmate moving to another city or state was delivered as though they had died. When Burney was in grade school, her family just moved to a better neighborhood across town, but a child doesn't have to change zip codes to face upheaval and disaster in a new crowd. A different street can do it.

The girl's on Sherwood Drive let her tag along with them or maybe behind them and, desperate to be accepted my mother agreed to whatever mischief was afoot.

Burney describes a game they played called 'Spin': "You paired off with a partner and took turns spinning each other around as fast as you could. Then you stopped suddenly, clasped your partner's chest and squeezed." "Were you trying to make them pass out?" I asked. "Not exactly, she said, but it was definitely an out of body experience." "I bet."

My mother remembers playing spin with her new, not quite friends and a partner named Clara. Clara wanted to spin but Burney was apprehensive and reluctant. The other girls chided her, laughing and calling her goody, goody and scaredy, scaredy—both of which she was. But in spite of her better angels, Burney succumbed to the pressure, grabbed Clara's hands and whirled her around.

She spun and spun, then she stopped abruptly, wrapped her arms around the girl's chest and squeezed. Clara suddenly collapsed to the floor, face down. Burney thought she'd killed her. Clara's face was bloody; she'd lost one tooth and dislodged another. The paramedics told the girls that if my mother had kept her grip a few seconds longer, Clara could have died.

Years later, long after they'd gone their separate ways into other neighborhoods and adulthood, Burney read in the Knoxville News Sentinel that Clara had been killed in a car accident. The newspaper account noted that she likely would have survived had she not been weakened by a collapsed lung in a childhood accident. She left behind her husband and two young children.

How easy it is for us to go from acting as agents of good to agents of ill, to ignore the sound thinking that sends up a caution but is quickly drowned out by louder voices promising success, relief, acceptance and belonging. We all bear this duality, this shadow and light, this treasure made of dirt.

I asked my mother how she was able to forgive herself and go on. She said:

"I don't know, I agonized over Clara but I knew it was an accident and I was eventually able to accept God's mercy and move forward."

I've wrestled with my own bad actions, the hurt I've caused, the things I can take responsibility for but cannot repair. In middle school my temper got the best of me at an ice skating party and I kicked a girl on the ice, splitting her shin and sending her to the emergency room for stitches.

My parents came to the party, a sleepover and took me home that night and I remember Burney in the door of my room, telling me, as she had told me before, she despaired over me at times. But by then, I didn't need anyone to despair over me, I carried so much shame I supplied my own misery and hopelessness. The King James version of Psalm 139 begins: "Oh Lord, thou hast searched me and known me, thou knowest my downsitting and mine uprising. Thou understandeth my thoughts afar off." I love the use of the word 'uprising', it perfectly describes my temper, my tempest, my ongoing revolt. It also reminds me that I am known and loved in full—tempest and all.

All of us do harm in this world, all of us "...could use some mercy now" as my friend Mary Gauthier writes in her song. We need it, we need to receive it and just as much, to give it. We know this so why is it so hard? Maybe Burney's fears that I was prison bound kept her saying anything and everything she thought would be harsh enough to get my attention. I know that feeling, I've done it with my own daughter, thinking if I just say it one more time, or this other way she will suddenly hear and turn. But she didn't, she ran, just like me.

The 9th of the 12th steps reads: "Made direct amends to such people (we had harmed) wherever possible except when to do so would injure them or others." The first time I 'did' my ninth step it felt like I was mea culpa-ing all over the world. Most people I had offended or hurt were generous and quick to forgive but there was one person who said bluntly: "No, I won't forgive you. You're an asshole." He's right about that—I have plenty of asshole in me—and I liked him for saying in essence: Not so fast....sit in it a while. A time out in the sorry seat can be transforming.

I started another ninth step a few years ago and realized I was current with everyone I knew of but one: me. I'd never forgiven myself for much of anything, never even tried really. I had also never forgiven myself for not forgiving myself. It felt good to keep an atonal flame, less good to let myself off the hook with acceptance and compassion. Sitting in that was an exercise in grief, grief over my life, my family, my losses, my rage that had caused such harm. I don't know that I can call myself transformed in this ongoing strictly spirit-led work but I can say that I've unclenched my fists and begun to accept the mercy I long to give.

Burney has softened in that area too. Once on a visit I confided my hateful, jealous feelings towards a family member to her. I don't typically do this, knowing that I'm likely to get a lecture and a bible verse. This time though she quietly laid her hand over mine and said, "I understand". It's a revelation to me how much healing those two words can contain.

PRACTICE

Mixing bitter with sweet, bringing our entire alphabet to the stage, is it worth all that? A tiny flaw, a pair of garden shears, emojipedia, a few shiny hearts and the fiber optic bridge closing the gap between us.

FILLING THE BUCKET

My friend Arthur Boers wrote a book, Living Into Focus with the subtitle, Choosing What Matters In An Age of Distraction. His premise was focal practice as a tool to bring balance into our stressed out lives. He points out the irony early on that: 'labor-saving' devices only make us busier, a fact I'm keenly aware of in the middle of the night when my husbands iWatch, iPad, iMac and iPhone all chirp and ding and chorus at once with work bulletins.

Arthur encourages us readers to retire our carpe diem posters and receive the days rather than seizing them. Replacing some of the manic over scheduled hyper-vigilance with pursuits that ask us to slow down and concentrate on the single task at hand creates mental space and harmony among other things. There are numerous examples of focal practice: walking, fishing, knitting, quilting, bird watching, praying, gardening, cooking, reading, playing an instrument, learning another language. The loss of many of these things in our lives has a lot to do with the time and effort they require and yet it is that kind of engagement that offers deeper fulfillment and teaches us to struggle well to attain something.

I'm fortunate to have been raised in a household where focal practice was a natural part of family life. When my sister Jennie and my brother Paul were young, my step-father Joe used to read aloud from Frank Baum's Oz books at night, populating their imaginations with characters that resembled spare parts from the junkyard. Burney has many focal practices, though I don't know she would call them that. She's simply looking for ways to elevate daily living into something less mundane and more memorable.

My mother gave no quarter to Sara Lee or Stouffer's at the dinner hour beyond fish sticks or a once in a while pot pie when she was working full time. She's always had gardens, arranged flowers and loved to read. But at the moment I'm thinking of blackberries.

Burney started blackberry picking as a child in The Great Smoky Mountains and it quickly became a summer family ritual. My grandfather Papa, an avid fly fisherman, was out on the water at dawn and began spotting large masses of undiscovered bushes along the Little River banks. He read up on jam and jelly making and led the berry picking expeditions. To remove the seeds he'd heap them in a pillowcase set over a bucket to drain overnight. He sterilized the jars and when the jelly was ready to set, he filled each clear container with sparkling amethyst colored fruit. Papa finished by sealing the jars with thin layers of melted paraffin, something my mother does to this day, dismissing modern canning techniques.

More recently, Burney dreamed up 'camp sunshine' for her grandchildren's summer visits to her home in El Dorado, California. In between the clamored over excursions to sports events in San Francisco and a local water park, she scouted the area for blackberry bushes and found several. Her favorite was near a stream by a local drive-in called the Shoestring where she could pick through the morning and then reward herself with a chili dog and a root beer float.

When my son Henry and my nephew Zach were middle schoolers they flew to California for ten days at Granny's. Zach loved the blackberry picking and later mentioned it as a highlight in a school paper called: "All About Me, A Brief History Of The Life Of Zach Yellen." Henry, on the other hand, remembers sitting on the curb wishing he had his Game Boy as he watched Granny in her long-sleeved shirt reaching for the fat little prizes and urging the boys to jump into the brambles. My mother said she provoked a moment of intense misery when she collected their electronics on arrival and kept them on a high shelf for the duration of their visit. But it was just a moment and all the grandchildren lined up for trips to camp sunshine and adventures with Granny, who Henry called 'the original party animal.'

California features excellent growing conditions and local growers with uncommon fruit. But Burney says she tried jam-making with berries she bought at the Farmers Market once and it wasn't the same. Commercial produce and even pre-picked local berries are uniformly ripe and miss the wild tang that comes from mixing berries of different readiness along with the slightly bitter seeds.

I am one that has tried to cull the bitter from my life as I've aged, seeking some safety in sameness and steering clear of the thorns. But all of creation declares the truth of God and I know, as much as I often don't want to know that there is life in the bitter, that the tang in the sweet is the capacity for joy that can only come by accepting and tasting that bitter to the full, that there is something deeply nourishing starting with an empty bucket and eventually, step by step, making my way to the table with something delicious in my hand to savor and share.

Berry picking is a spring and summer pastime in Tennessee. I occasionally make trips to a little spot south of Franklin filled with hundreds of blueberry bushes and though I tire of it fairly quickly in the humidity, I do like feeling outside of time for a little while as I concentrate on each bush and filling my bucket. It feels like childhood when the days stretched endlessly before me and idle hours were meant to be filled with tadpoles from the creek and exploring or sprawled in the grass looking for a four leaf clover. Children do not generally need to practice being present, that is where they live. It is adulthood that lands us in the past or the future or anywhere but here—and now.

The current 'here and now' is a tough one. I have thought often of how I will emerge from this pandemic. What will I return to? What will I consign to pre-corona days? I have deeply appreciated the enforced simplicity of this time, the small space I inhabit and the focus on a few things done slowly and deliberately each day. Dag Hammerskjold writes of the "...point of rest at the center of our being..." which to me describes our internal focal point, the place we sometimes reach in the quiet effort, the contemplation and concentration as well as the mistakes and frustration. Always there is bitter and sweet.

I ask Burney about her own philosophical reflections stirred in these practices. She answers: "Well, I like the idea of God's abundance by the side of the road free for the taking and the memories are part of it too, but my main thought is: how can I reach that branch full of juicy berries without keeling over or getting scratched?" No doubt she'll find a way.

MOMENT OF GLORY

Years ago my brother-in-law, Mitch, driven by a love of acting and theater, decided to stage a fund raising production of The Sound Of Music in
Petaluma, California where several members of my family were living. He
approached Burney about playing the part of Reverend Mother. She said
no initially, feeling that her flutey soprano was too thin and not up to the
task and that the great performances she'd watched on stage and screen
would dominate her thoughts and intimidate her from delivering her own
best work. Mitch persisted, dangling an irresistible carrot of opportunity to
act alongside some of her grandchildren and she ultimately relented. Burney auditioned for the role and got it immediately, owing to the fact she
says that no one else tried out for it. Nevertheless, it was a part she was
born to play.

My mother unashamedly loves spectacle and the spotlight though she is
equally enthusiastic whether as a performer or an audience member. She
was obsessively devoted to American Idol for many years and expressed
surprise and disappointment when I refused to watch and evaluate with her.
Burney said: "You're in the music business, I can't believe you don't like
this show." I told her American Idol was about being a star, not an artist and
she looked at me as if to say: 'Exactly'.

Burney kept careful track of each contestant, their back stories, hits and

143

misses each week and reported to me who she thought was worthy of the crown at the end of the season. She was thrilled one year when a singer from Miami shocked us all by singing a song my husband Kenny and I had written and recorded. It was not a particularly well known song and a brave choice on a show that trades mostly in classic material and big hits. Of course, once I had a contender, in no time at all I was fully tuned in, involved in the voting and nail biting over the judges reaction.

The singer, Nadia Turner, was the big winner the night she performed our song, Power Of Love, getting nods not only for a great vocal but also for stepping outside the box with an obscure choice of material. I remained devoted to the show until the night Nadia was eliminated and then resumed my shunning. Burney carried on and continued to report the highlights every year.

I was traveling for work during the Petaluma run of The Sound Of Music and unable to attend any of the shows but Burney said they'd made a good video and on my next visit we sat down to watch it together. My mother sat in a chair directly in front of the tv, easily inhabiting the role of Reverend Mother. At the end of Act 1 in her crowning performance of Climb Ev'ry Mountain, I looked over and realized she was weeping as she watched.

In the interest of fairness and full disclosure I too have been moved to tears by my own good work. I know when I first finish writing a song if it stirs my emotions and fills my eyes, I'm likely onto something good.

'Performance' is a loaded word for many of us who grew up in a family or sector of society where it was a given expectation to demonstrate our worth. My parents were both natural performers in every part of their lives. I didn't feel like I had any worth to demonstrate but I found I could excel in negative performance, which I did, until I discovered a gift for music and shortly after that, the stage. Here was an unexpected place of refuge where I could be alone in the crowd—something I was familiar and comfortable with. It was easy to be at ease separated on an elevated platform—much harder on the floor.

There is a space where we occupy our gifts—whatever they may be—that

144

is not quite as arrogant or self-seeking—or even self-protective, but God given and God ordained. This idea is echoed in the memorable comment made by Eric Liddell in Chariots of Fire: "I believe God made me for a purpose, but he also made me fast. And when I run I feel His pleasure." I have felt it too—the trick is recognizing that skinny line between employing my abilities as an expression of pleasure and gratitude and using them in hopes that people will love and admire me. Maybe it's impossible to separate the two, maybe that's part of the gift—the human part.

I smiled watching my mother tearfully relive her moment of glory on the local Casa Grande Middle School stage and had an epiphany. I typically associate performance Burney with other B led words: bold, bullet-proof, beautiful, brazen, but here was a softer consonant. She is vulnerable—just like me—when it comes to demonstrating her worth and I felt the love and kinship that emerges from recognition, like a sigh of relief: you too?

We bring our entire alphabet to the stage. Most of us put in the woodshed hours and feel more or less prepared but at some point the only way to deliver is to forget what we know and step into the moment. On a good night I feel weightless and free. On a bad one, I can plan on little or no sleep. But for those of us who are made for it—like me, like Burney—the pull is greater than any risk. Who knows, maybe we'll traipse among the stars tonight and deliver something sob worthy.

A COMPLICATED LIFE

At 88, Burney declares her doing is very nearly done. But it isn't, not very, not nearly, not done. Consider compost. I never know what I'll find my mother up to when I visit but I know she'll be up to something. Last time it was empty half gallon ice cream cartons she had stationed in her kitchen, on the patio and in the garage ready and waiting for ...what? I asked her. She said: "I have a recipe that's supposed to set your garden, well not on fire but bursting with color and growth and bounty." "Bounty? Mom, what century are you in?" That's the question with Burney, she likes the tedium of another age, one that included outhouses. She tells me she's collected dried banana peels, coffee grounds and carefully washed and dried egg shells to mix in a grinder. "You own a grinder?" I ask "Well, no and I don't think my blender is up to the task but I have a Ninja that works pretty well so I'll try that." I suggest a mortar and pestle and she rolls her eyes.

I ask my mother: "Is it worth all this?" She says: "Well, so far there's not much action on my part—it's all happening in my mind." I peek into one of her many containers and there are the desiccated banana peels, looking pitifully like other small blackened dead things in advanced decomposition. Burney says she knows some people wouldn't have a problem just abandoning the whole operation and buying a bag of Miracle Gro (me, for

147

instance). She can't say yet if it works since she hasn't finished cooking her compost but, she assures me, " I'm moving ever closer."

My youngest daughter Lily lived with Burney one summer and reported her idiosyncrasies to me regularly. "Granny puts her paper towels in the washing machine. She takes forever to do anything or get anywhere because everything has to be done a certain way. She has stacks of books, magazines and note pads all over her house and writes notes to herself on scraps of paper. But then she loses them under other scraps of paper." Over time though, Lily noticed things my mother did that inspired her, hand writing thank you notes (sometimes in reply to thank you notes), sitting down to her meals even when she ate alone, giving thanks and actually tasting the food, warming her plates, keeping a familiar era and its practices alive.

Burney says she knows she sounds like a typical old lady surrounded by equally old tables covered in doilies with crumbs under them and dusty books. I tell her she's anything but typical but my mother is off and running now: "I know I complicate my life. Neel used to ask me why I do all these things that exhaust me and I said, because I think they're important. She'd laugh and say, 'Not me, I just want to watch soaps." That wasn't entirely true. My cousin Neel did love her soaps but she also learned a few things while she lived with my mother, particularly regarding cooking and entertaining, things she had no previous training or confidence in. Neel had an apartment for a time in the Portrero Hill neighborhood of San Francisco. It was the first place she'd rented that she wanted to invite people to and managed a dinner party with lamb curry and a salad that my mother had coached her on and assured her of success. Neel crowed about her party for years and told anyone in earshot that whatever domestic skills she had, she'd learned from her aunt Burney. I learned from Burney too—though I needed 2300 miles and my own household to step into those skills. My mothers watchful eye was connected to a swift pair of hands, ready to demonstrate a better alternative to my early clumsy attempts. I knew she was right but I hated the hovering.

Now Burney is onto one of her top five recurring topics, church potlucks. "In my day, a woman's reputation as a hostess and a cook and a community member were on the line at church socials but now everybody brings a Costco salad and we're lucky if they open the bag before they plop it on the table." She has taken it upon herself to leap into the fray of this gross etiquette breach with recipes and elbow grease. She tells me of a painstaking recipe for asparagus that involves carefully puncturing the spears to release water, dipping each spear in egg whites that have been beaten into soft peaks and finally rolling them, again, one at a time, in a mixture of panko crumbs and parmesan before baking them. Needless to say, she did not allow herself enough prep time (I'm guessing a whole day) and was late to the potluck. Finally after carefully arranging her creation in a pretty green dish and grabbing her silver tongs, she swept into the church fellowship hall and found a spot among the salad bags. Once again the recurring question: "Was it worth all that?" She says, "I assume so—it looked and smelled delicious but I never got a chance to try it, every asparagus was gone by the time I got to the table."

I, for one, am grateful that a woman's reputation as a community member is no longer dependent on the quality of her covered dishes but I understand and share some of my mother's sentiment. I, too, take the long view, preferring hand written letters and time consuming recipes, not always, but often. I do it for a mix of reasons and though the results are not always superior, there is still joy in the doing and I learn some little tweak I didn't know before. We were made for the slow detailed work of creating, one word or ingredient at a time. And though I love shortcuts as well as anyone, there's satisfaction for me in slow—not just in the outcome but in the mistakes, the love, the discovery, and yes, the tedium. Is it worth all that? Yes, it is.

I tell my mother to stop dwelling on the stuff she is not so gifted at: organization, for instance, and focus on receiving the delight that others take in many of her practices. She views her paper flooded home as a liability, Lily sees it as active combat against the death of print and something to hold onto. And somewhere in that stack is a pretty piece of stationary that Burney will fill with carefully printed, carefully chosen words and she'll find a stamp and get it mailed to a carefully chosen recipient and that person will know someone else in the world thought enough of them to drop what they were doing, take a seat and take the time to put it in writing.

THROUGH THE GARDEN GATE

Burney and her sister Betsy had a game they called 'Corsage'. They combed the alley behind their house for flowers and plants with strict instructions from their mother that they could only take the stray vines and blooms that escaped their neighbors fences and gates. The girls returned home loaded down with whatever was growing and using small shoeboxes from the endless supply at my grandfathers store, Poll Parrott Shoes, created tiny bouquets in nests of tissue paper.

"Sounds very Victoriana." I said asking my mother: "Was it a competition?" "No, it was a game. But it was my game and my rules and I don't remember what I did to get Betsy to play it with me but her corsages were always messy and thrown together so I don't think she had the same passion for it that I did." "Who decided on a winning bouquet?" I asked. "I did" answered Burney. "So...you were creator, implementor and judge?" "Well, yes" she said. "That might explain Betsy's lack of enthusiasm."

Burney who packs her suitcases with tissue paper between items of clothing took equal pains in every tiny detail of her corsages and assures me she deserved the crown(s). Once the bouquets were complete, they tied them with bits of ribbon, my mother excelling here as well, carefully producing—as she puts it—an even, crisp bow.

151

"It's a sweet picture, don't you think" she asked? "It's a little fussy for me" I said. "and also—who knew the sinister heights you would take it to in adulthood?"

Burney is a stickler, not just with blossoms and bows, she's liable to stickle anywhere and especially with propriety. She bemoans the loss of civility, refined manners and gracious conduct along with good grammar in all areas of life. And yet.

I have clear memories of my mother leaving the house in the morning or after dark for her constitutional walks with a small pair of garden shears tucked in her pocket. Sometimes she wore canvas gloves, sometimes she left her gall at home—but most times she returned with an armload of flowers grown elsewhere. Not only did she reach over and under fences, she walked right through gates into gardens belonging to people she knew and people she did not know, relieving them of a few sprigs here and a few there. When I suggested she was stealing she dismissed me with a small wave: "Oh they don't care." "How would you know unless you asked them?"

The imaginative romance of corsages and nosegays in my mother's childhood developed into a formidable gift for flower arranging in adulthood. Often her raids were prompted by a request from her church to adorn the altar on Sunday morning or for a special event hosted by someone for whom the cost of a florist would have been prohibitive. That made her mission holy and she assumed that any reasonable person would be more than happy to donate a bit of their landscaping for a good cause but I don't recall that she actually knocked on anybody's door to ask if she could denude a rose bush.

I wonder aloud how she excuses these little thefts and she laughs and says: "Well, perhaps it is a flaw in my character but really just a tiny one and I always cut expertly and judiciously." "Well that changes everything" I say. "I guess there's no point in reciting: "good fences make good neighbors."

My aunt Marion asked Burney to make the table centerpieces for an event prior to her daughter Elizabeth's wedding and they decided on topiaries. My mother flew from San Francisco to Greensboro, North Carolina with curly willow sticks, smilax and other bits of greenery in her carry on. During the flight a woman seated behind her tapped her on the shoulder and said there were ants crawling down her back. She responded airily "Oh, I'm not surprised". I think there are agricultural laws about interstate travel with plants now, possibly related to this incident.

When she arrived in Greensboro, Burney told Marion they needed roses but not the stiff, newly opened buds found at the florists. She wanted something soft and full, like the heavy petaled antique roses. Marion told her, "Burney, I don't know where we're going to find anything like that." "Well, surely you know someone with a rose garden."

Marion thought for a minute and replied her boss had beautiful roses. "Great!"enthused my mother. "Let's go!"

"Burney, I'm not going to sneak into my bosses yard with you to cut his flowers."

Burney told her sister that she would do the cutting, Marion just needed to drive the get away car. I asked her if Marion's boss was invited to the party "No, it was the bridesmaid's luncheon but he wouldn't have noticed if he had been there." "Why? How many roses did you take?" "I don't remember but let's just say they were beautiful topiaries."

I am no one to talk. My tastes lean to wildflowers and I'm more likely to bring home moss and lichen. But I am partial to Virginia bluebells and when they dot the hillsides in early spring at Edwin Warner park, I usually finish my walk with a few stalks from the side of the road concealed in my coat. Sometimes I have a small moment of dread imagining having a heart attack and the EMTs discovering my illegal loot when they tear open my jacket to resuscitate. But it passes quickly and does little to dampen my enthusiasm for the little blue lavender bell-shaped blooms that spill over the lip of a small vase in my kitchen window and gladden my heart. I see the signs posted at Edwin Warner, I know there are laws against wild flower picking in public parks and I understand why they are needed. I have no argument or justification. Sometimes my desire to live transparently and uprightly prompts me to keep my hands to myself; sometimes not.

153

Frankly, there's no limit to my need for mercy in my daily displays of selfishness. But if I am to receive forgiveness, I must surely extend it, even and especially to those rule-breakers who happen to be ignoring the ones I like to keep.

The other day I was on a trail in the same park and noticed one of my pet irritations, a gaily colored plastic bag of dog poop, neatly tied and left helpfully on the side of the trail or hanging from a tree branch, for the maid I suppose. I see these nearly every time I walk or hike, left on the roadside day after day until some samaritan hiker picks them up and deposits them in a garbage can. I see them and I fume: 'Just wait until I catch one of the idiots doing this'. Then I remember the bluebells and try to let it go—or even better, pick up the bag and throw it away.

"Be kind, for everyone you meet is fighting a hard battle" is a popular quote attributed to the Scotsman, Reverend John Watson, also known as Ian Maclaren. Overlooking an offense, large or small is not my strong suit, not even with myself but I recognize that we all, every one, could use a pass on any given day.

On a recent trip to South Carolina my mother commented on the Spanish moss hanging from the trees and said she might like to take some home with her. We were on the grounds of a public plantation and I noticed some of the silvery moss lying in the grass. You could probably tuck that in your purse I said. She replied, "Oh that's not my style, I like to do my clipping after dark." 'She's not even sorry' I thought.

LOVE LETTERS

The sculptor, William Edmondson talked of standing in his driveway and seeing The Lord hang a tombstone in the sky 'right there in the noon daylight'. He said God called him by name and told him to pick up his tools and start cutting. I don't know if The Lord similarly suspended a fleecy valentine box in the heavens to inspire Burney but she says she had an immediate vision when she was awarded the task of transforming a lowly cardboard container for her grammar school class party. She wrapped her box in ruffled crepe paper, using streamers to create rosettes and anchoring her fancy touches with a red paper heart.

February 14th landed that year along with snow on the ground in Knoxville and my mother panicked that school would be canceled and she would be stuck at home with her lovely creation and no one to admire it. Fortunately the city fired up what had to have been their only snowplow and the roads were swept clean just in time for the first bell. Burney strode confidently through the classroom door, valentine box in hand and into a life devoted to the art of presentation. She was a girly girl then, she is a girly girl now, always on the lookout for an opportunity to elevate the ordinary with beauty and a few shiny hearts.

155

She sent a valentine to Kenny and me this year, expressing her love and appreciation for us. At one time it would have been a careful creation of lace, paper doilies, old fashioned stickers of cherubs and heartfelt sentiment. Now, she has far too many people on her love list to produce a special snowflake of a card for each so she contents herself with store bought elaborate pop up designs and confines her decor to the sentiment, written in ribbons of words that are warm and personal.

She may have put away her craft box but she has found the emoji button on her phone and sends mini-valentines to her nearest and dearest throughout any given day. Once she mistakenly sent me a text meant for her grandson Abe who had just left for the airport following a visit. She told him she missed him already, that he had no idea what his stay meant to her, that she loved him very, very much. She kept her comments brief and let emojipedia do the signifying, surrounding each tender declaration with sobbing sad faces at Abe's departure and hearts galore.

I too am a fan of things handmade and handwritten and though I'm not a girly girl, I have my own valentine box full of scraps of ribbon, lace, wrapping paper and stickers. I prevailed upon my children as soon as they could hold a pencil to express their affection and gratitude tangibly with notes that actually said something other than, "Thank you for the gift" or, "How are you? I am fine." It's the personal that supplies meaning. People say, 'I can't write like you can' and I argue that the eloquence and intimacy are in the specifics.

My husband, Kenny measures his speech; he says little and often when the emotion runs high he says nothing at all. When I ask him how he feels about something, he'll respond with "I don't know. It's hard to put into words." "Try" I say with no small amount of frustration. But most of the time when I press him, I come up empty. He is a man of letters though, cards to be specific and does not fail to mark every occasion with an envelope or two on my placemat at breakfast. The cards run the gamut: funny, sexy, sappy. I especially like the Hallmark grand gestures with WIFE embossed in gold letters across the front. We declare the miracle of our many years together frequently. But regardless of the type of card, it's the handful of words, barely legible, scrawled inside and kept between us that tell me his whole heart. I use the cards as bookmarks and return to them again and again to be reminded that I am known and loved by one very good man.

How essential it is to be told that we are cherished and on the heart and mind of another. But it is not only that we are cared for, it is the awareness that someone else delights in us. I love the Westminster catechism definition of human purpose: "The chief end of man is to glorify God and enjoy Him forever." We are made not only to honor and glorify God but to relish his company just as he does ours. Consider the 139th Psalm, a valentine if ever there was one:

How precious also are Your thoughts to me O God!

How great is the sum of them!

If I should count them they would be more in number than the sand;

When I awake, I am still with You.

(NKJV verses 17-18)

But as important as it is to say what's on our hearts, if there is no verb substance, the sentiment is empty. I had a friend who sent texts out of the blue: "I've been thinking about you, I miss you." I'd respond in kind and ask: "When can we go for a walk together?" Then—nothing. She'd ask me to do something for her and after I did, she'd follow up with a profusion of superlatives and text: "I'm sending you something as a deep thanks." Then— nothing. She'd tell me she was excited to celebrate my birthday then cancel at the last minute with a text: "I have a gift, I'll drop it by." Then—nothing. I hadn't asked her for any of this but once she declared she was going to do something, an expectation landed on the table. When I saw her, no mention was ever made and eventually I went well beyond annoyance into 'I never want to see you again' apathy.

Not so with Burney. She backs up every emoji heart or sob with presence. As I've said before, I don't always get what I want and sometimes I get more than I want, but I know she's ready to give what she has faithfully. In essence this book began as a valentine to my mother, to let her know that as water flowed under the bridge, the love sailed on and that even a leaky boat can take you on a great ride.

Maybe this year I'll send valentines randomly, regardless of the month or day, just to do it, to let someone know I take great pleasure in the fact of them. If I do, I'll deliver them in person.

HELLO!

When I close the 2300 miles between Burney and me with a direct flight and a good book, I look forward to our visits though inevitably somewhere in the packing is a question mark. How will it go?

I don't know that I will ever fully resolve the ambivalence I feel towards my mother. At times I love her wildly, at times I can't get a bit in my mouth fast enough I'm so irritated. I expect my own children endure similar love and grief with me. Love and grief, wounds and nurture, words that heal, words that don't, this is the book of family.

Sometimes face to face is unavailable—sometimes unadvisable—but through this process of learning my mothers life in detail, I've found sturdiness in the fiber optic bridge that clears the miles and closes the gap between us.

Burney gives great telephone. Whereas in person she can be distant and pre-occupied, critical or pushing her Pollyanna-isms, once she finds her phone, she is usually present and attentive. My aunt Marion says every time she calls Burney with a reason, she ends up in Candyland on a winding path so colorful and amusing, everything else, including her reason, is forgotten.

Once I called my mother and got an earful about a 'comedy' fashion show she was hosting and providing commentary for at her church. She'd been planning her costume for the event—initially thinking she would take the podium as Barbara Bush, draped in shrubbery and a collar of pearls. Until, that is, her fiddle leaf ficus tree waved its giant leaves at her—and her imagination. Burney enthused: "I just needed a flesh tone unitard, my snake skin sandals and three leaves—one for my crotch, one for the crack in the back and one for my flat little bosom". Enter Eve.

As my own children have flown I keep them close with speed dial. We talk about our lives, what's happening in the world and on tv, deep things, hard things, good things and nothing at all. Lily and I rarely talk less than an hour, Henry's attention span is a bit shorter. But the connections are there, strong and satisfying. Not so with Rebecca, who long ago put miles and drugs between us. Years go by with little or no contact and I wonder if anything happened to her, would anyone let me know? Just when I feel the tiny flame of hope I carry for my first born begin to gutter, I'll pick up the phone, dial or text—and she'll break the San Francisco fog of silence with: "Mom, I'm just walking out the door, I'll call you in a little while, I promise." I know she won't but just hearing her voice, the fact of her, is enough to put me back on a path of faith. I also know that a longer conversation would be upsetting. Becca would tell me what she knows I want to hear—assurances of a return to sober living. But I would hear what I don't want to hear: the lies, the insanity that radiates from the disease and the disease itself, working me. So I thank God for those brief exchanges that tell me the only thing I really want to know—she's alive.

When the corona pandemic began, I developed an immediate rash for Zoom. I was distracted by my picture—the 'covid casual' look of I don't care. The nuance of face to face and body language was lost in small one-dimensional squares that suffered time delays and poor lighting. But as the months drag on, I realize that these connections—full of holes, just like with in the flesh, keep me tied to community and remind me that there is affirmation to be found, even in the most wanting interaction.

Thinking over all the conversations with Burney these last few years—more than in the twenty before—and all the stories that have bonded us and enlarged my perspective of who I am and where I came from, I understand that one of the best gateway words in the world, spoken in person or fit into a mouthpiece is: Hello!

160

HOSPITALITY

A viewfinder with a wider lens, why are all these people here? A meal, a lap, acceptance and some version of the word 'cat' for a name, a good life, a good death and a misplaced messiah complex.

STORY SHAPED

My sister Jennie sent me a text: "If you haven't heard mom's latest story about going to a new acquaintance's home for dinner, you need to call her. Good stuff." Burney can make a story out of anything. I don't think she plans or develops them, I think she embodies them. I called and asked about her dinner. My mother described her hostess calling her days in advance and telling her excitedly she'd been cooking up a storm. She said the woman was standing outside waiting for her when she arrived and carefully instructed her how to park her car. Then, apparently not satisfied, asked for the keys and told my mother she would park her car. This would have been enough for me to shift into reverse but Burney gamely complied.

'Cooking up a storm' as it turns out produced spaghetti squash with a "… strange pink sauce, minced broccoli with a blob of mayonnaise and a piece of bread topped with a single slice of Velveeta". Burney surveyed her plate, picked up her fork and said, "This looks delicious." I don't know that the evening was a howling success for either woman but my mother sensed her acquaintance was lonely and she was glad she spent some time with her.

For me, Burney's gift with story is not so much that she knows how to tell them—though she surely does—but the fact that she willingly enters the stories of others. All of us are entertained by good story—and conversely, all of us know what it is to be taken hostage by someone who drones on and on with mind numbing details that bloat sentences into misery for the listeners. I recall my father in law once devoting 20 minutes to telling me how cardboard boxes were made.

Burney's viewfinder has a wider lens. She recognizes the great need for connection and compassionate listening and is willing to entertain pretty much anyone's story, good or bad. She is, of course, better at this with strangers than her flesh and blood and I who have a lifelong need to go beyond nonfiction into confession learned the hard way, over and over that not every story needs to be told—especially to my mother.

But tell her I did and when I told Burney the one thing she least wanted to hear, that I was alone, unmarried, unattached, alcoholic, drug addicted, and pregnant, to my surprise, she took up residence in my story, right in the middle of the mess.

My father, my family, my friends, my church all stepped in to help and provide whatever support they could. But my mother stepped the farthest, crossing the gaping divide of her hopes and dreams for me and her first grandchild into a stark reality. She ignored the reaction of some in her community and set aside the conservative principles she holds dear, to come alongside me, not entirely without critical comment—she's still Burney—but mostly with encouragement on her lips. She volunteered to be my Lamaze partner and took walks with me, pep-talking her way down the block, she smoothed the path to telling my grandparents and best of all, when I told her I wanted to keep my baby she tearfully declared that was her hearts desire too.

I know she 'done it for love' but I didn't know she 'done it' because she too had been the recipient of the generosity shaped by dying to our selves until we started these conversations.

My great grandmother Bessie was considered a beloved saint in Greenwood, the county seat of South Carolina. My mother said one of Bessie's few points of pride was the fact that no one in her family had ever been to jail or gotten divorced. "Good thing she didn't live to see you end the stay

164

out of jail streak." Burney said to me laughing. "Thanks mom."

Mama—or great mama as we called her, lived out her marriage commitment at great personal cost. The relentless progression of my great grandfather Edwards' alcoholism brought regular strain and heartache to their relationship. The bond finally snapped when their youngest son Hayes was born and Edward was nowhere to be found. When he finally appeared, galloping into the yard on his horse and saw his son for the first time, he slurred drunkenly to my great grandmother, "I don't know whose son he is but he is surely not mine." Great mama said later the offense cut so deep she was never able to forgive him and she never let him in her bed again either. But she kept her commitment to stay married for better and all the worse that followed until the day he died.

I don't recall ever having a conversation with Edward or great papa. By the time I came along, he was a shadowy figure in a rocking chair on the front veranda, smoking a pipe, drinking whiskey and muttering "ho hum". He presided over each meal at the head of the dining room table with his hair parted, wetted and combed to the side, but never said much. Late at night he had plenty to say and could be heard in a back bedroom shouting obscene demands for sex until he passed out. Bessie had a thriving business as a seamstress and was, for many years, the primary bread winner of the house but I don't think it ever occurred to her that she had options regarding her marriage. She made her choice and that was that.

When Burney came to the end of her own marriage she says the person she most dreaded telling was Bessie. She agonized over every word in a letter she wrote to her grand mother, knowing she was mailing disappointment to someone she adored.

When the telephone rang a week or so later, Burney picked up the receiver and heard:

"Dahlin, I am lovin you so much right now." My mother cries in the telling, knowing what it cost my great grandmother to set aside the propriety she would not have surrendered for her own happiness. Bessie added in her musical drawl she was going to send my mother a little folding money and

165

shortly after that a check for $1,000 arrived. A thousand dollars is a substantial gift any time but in those days, it was a kings ransom, every dollar, an hour, sewing and embroidering.

I began this book with the idea of story. I knew my mother would deliver and enliven these pages. What I didn't know was that there was medicine in those tales and that my own lens would expand with understanding and connection. That's the beauty of listening—often we emerge with more than we gave.

Just as during the pandemic, people in Wuhan noticed the birdsong as the great noise of engines died down, in the quiet as we hear the pieces of one another's days, the laments, the loves and longings, we are likely to discover new notes in the songs of our own lives.

WALL TO WALL WELCOME MAT

Late in life, Burney and my step-father, Joe moved to the foothills of the Sierras near a town called Placerville. Placerville, or Hangtown, as the locals call it, is pure Steinbeck California and sits on the snow line just below the Sierra Mountains. My parents found a sprawling property with a ranch house, a barn, a view and Llamas standing at the fence of the farm down the road.

My mother likes a daily dose of AA and found an early morning meeting shortly after the move. She sat in the clubhouse among the well heeled and newly paroled. She gripped her coffee cup with manicured hands and shared her life alongside all different kinds of men and women, many of whom were sleeved head to toe with tattoos and utterly lacking in the smallest social grace.

Every year when the holidays came around Burney hosted a party for the members of her AA group. She received them as honored guests and served them using her good silver and linen along with her prodigious cooking skills. After dinner she read two of her favorite Christmas stories as they gathered around her like children, spellbound. She is welcoming to the chic and familiar; she is welcoming to kinfolk; she is welcoming to the stranger and the strange; she is welcoming to those whom good sense would likely dictate otherwise.

167

Joe complained often about her open door policy saying: "Why are all these people here?" But he rarely came between Burney and her invitations, though he continued asking: "When are all these people leaving?" long after dementia had settled into his mind and the house was empty.

I don't think my mother could have turned anyone away. And it wasn't charity on her part, thank goodness, because an air of duty will steal the heart from the most noble intentions. She is genuinely interested in and entertained by people from all walks of life and enjoys a wide variety of company.

Burney brought in a number of people to live with us throughout my childhood, including our housekeepers. One, a small wiry woman named Tempe was selective about her tasks and excelled in negotiating what she would and would not do. My stepfather was an attorney and had a few negotiating skills himself. On occasions when he would out-maneuver Tempe and get his way, she would grudgingly comply but not without a few last words out of his earshot and directed at my mother. She would mutter a few indistinct comments that became louder and clearer as she warmed to her topic:

"When you work for regular folks they say: 'We need to talk'. But when you work for a lawyer, he'll say: 'Tempe, I'd like to schedule a conference.'" This would be followed by a long pause. Then she would turn to my mother as if she had just noticed her in the room and say: "Miz Sheeks, you ever notice how bow-legged Mr Sheeks is? Whoee he bout the bow-leggedest man I ever did see. Mmm hmm, he sure is".

Tempe came to my mother at one point and told her that her grandson, Tyrone desperately needed to get out of Detroit. The only influences surrounding Tyrone in the Motor City were bad ones and Tempe told my mother he need a fresh start and a good home—their home as a matter of fact. Joe expressed grave misgivings but my mother didn't hesitate and within days Tyrone was on a Greyhound making his way west.

Tyrone was handsome and well-mannered, Tempe was overjoyed and newly cooperative. All went smoothly—for a while. But eventually circum-

168

stances came to light and policemen came to the door. Tyrone was brought up on charges for crimes committed back in Detroit. Tempe was a wreck but her household sparring partner Joe stepped in offering to help and when Tyrone's trial came up, Tempe liked to say his representation had been secured Pro Buono by the bow-leggedest man in Northern California.

Tyrone got off with a light sentence and parole. He moved out shortly after that with Tempe following close behind. Burney shook out her welcome mat, ignoring Joe's pleas and protests and started scouting for the next guest room resident. I think of all the people that have crossed my mother's threshold and into her heart. But it wasn't only Burney. As much as he complained and tried to raise his voice of reason, sooner or later, Joe gave up and went with it. He surrendered his heart too in his own curmudgeonly way and to me, that was the more precious hospitality. My mother was simply doing what she was born to do, what she loves to do. Joe endured chaos and upheaval to his core and sacrificed his need for peace, quiet and routine. I imagine he went to his grave wondering: "When are all these people leaving?"

It's true that people often marry their opposites; Burney and Joe are great examples of that. I wonder if there's something instinctual in us that draws us to a person possessing the strengths we lack. These differences can be thorns no doubt but at their best they create balance and enlarge our borders. My friends Terry and Sharon Hargrave call this 'Us-ness'. They say: "Terry doesn't particularly like the ballet—but 'us' does. It's who we are together."

Burney tells me she's begun to roll up her welcome mat due to lack of space and plumbing. I smile thinking Joe would have liked to have seen that. But, maybe not, maybe he would have gotten what he wanted and found it diminishing. Maybe he would have started asking: "Where are all the people?"

169

WILD CATS

Maybe it started with my grandfather. Papa Parrott was fascinated by exotic animals and occasionally brought one home. There was a small monkey who declined to eat bananas, only the tiny seeds, scooping them out with its delicate fingers and tossing aside the squished flesh and peel. There was a baby alligator that a friend (?) had shipped from Florida. It was housed temporarily in a bathtub. But while the family considered a more suitable home, it disappeared. "In the house?" I ask. "Well, yes, says Burney. Rosabelle nearly quit over that one." "I'm with Rosabelle". I ask my mother if they found it but she doesn't remember. I tell her: "I would remember."

The Parrotts had a parrot that only said: "Polly want a cracker" incessantly—and a myna with better social skills including sound effects like: "Hello father, mother got a cold" accompanied by a discreet cough. Burney never went in for exotics as far as I know but her open door policy extended to animals and, in particular, cats, some of them feral.

My sister Windsor brought home Leo, a little black and white kitten who alienated my stepfather Joe early on by hopping up on the dinner table and polishing off a stick of butter while Burney was in the kitchen. Joe said Leo had to go and my mother advised Windsor to create a letter of apology with a paw print that went something like: Dear Mr. Sheeks: I apologize for my appetite which caused me to lose control and eat all of your butter. Mea Culpa. Love Leo Leo stayed.

'Mama Cat' a nondescript mottled gray showed up at our door alone but with the swollen nipples of recently delivery. We never found the kittens but the name stuck. Leo had gone to his reward and my stepfather, thinking he was free at last, tried to discourage adopting another feline "I don't like cats." He declared. My mother responded with the purchase of a litter box and food and Mama Cat moved in. Burney said she saw Joe petting her and talking to her when he thought no one was looking.

But the real evidence Joe had accepted and embraced Mama Cat was when he found her lying dead in the road hit by a car. He brought the sad news home and then took a pillow case and a shoe box to gather her remains. He and my mother walked across the bridge that led to the far side of their property, dug a hole and performed a brief ceremony, singing hymns and eulogizing Mama Cats independent spirit.

They were returning to the house when who should come strolling across the bridge without a care in the world but Mama Cat. Joe was flummoxed and wondered dumbly: "Who is that?" Burney said: "It would appear to be Mama Cat." "But who did we bury?" "Beats me. But we can rest in the fact we gave it a Christian burial"

In El Dorado, 'Kitty' arrived at the door one day, wild and wily. She was a gorgeous orange marmalade but had recently been in a fight or a trap and one leg was wounded and stripped of fur. My parents tried to get the leg treated, setting a dish of raw chicken inside a cat carrier for a trip to the vet. But Kitty's freedom was hard won and she rejected all confinement, even for her own good. If they tried to catch her, she bit and scratched. If they tried to pet her, she bit and scratched.

Kitty kept the upper paw in all things. On the rare occasions she wanted attention, she'd flop down beside them and purr loudly but it was always on her terms. Once she showed up with an infection in her eye from a foxtail and it took both my parents tag teaming, one holding Kitty in a towel, one spraying drops in the general vicinity of her eye while she ducked, bobbed and spat.

Kitty left one night, presumably to hunt and never returned. Burney and Joe both mourned her loss and probable demise but I think, took comfort in the idea that she likely died as she lived, still on her own terms.

After that, the house was quiet until one day my mother heard mewling coming from behind the wall. This seemed a bit much—cats everywhere. Joe dismissed it easily as one often does when they have begun to lose their hearing. But the cries continued and when Joe too finally heard it they brought someone in to investigate. He cut a hole in the wall and discovered a little blue-eyed kitten. No one had the slightest idea how it got there. Maybe word had made its way up and down Northern California among the members of felis catus there was a haven to be had at Burney and Joes. There, with no obligation, they'd be given a meal, a lap, acceptance and some version of the word 'cat' for a name. Who wouldn't show up?

I often hear faith in Christ referred to as a crutch but I think of it as home. Here I too have been loved and accepted even when I steal the butter, even when I bite and scratch. Here I have been given a name that tells me I am known. Here I have a refuge.

Personally, I love a good crutch. Food, drugs, alcohol, men and Marlboros are just a few of the props I've used to make this world habitable for me. But in Jesus I continue to find freedom and the ability to take life as it comes without something to temper it with, to be human without apology and to receive the place at the table that is offered me every day. And just like at Burney and Joes, all I have to do is show up.

GIVE IT AWAY, ALL OF IT

My mother joined a little prayer group at her church that meets weekly but they keep the prayer chain humming with text requests every day, all day long. I would tolerate this for, oh, I don't know, maybe ten minutes, having developed a hair trigger about group texting. Not Burney—she loves it. She clutches that little phone in anticipation and gets teary over nearly every petition. They are messages from the heart, messages of community and commitment, messages of sharing in the burdens that overwhelm the world. Burney hears the familiar chirp, stops what she's doing and devotes herself to the cry on the screen, often to the annoyance of whoever she's with—me, for instance. But then I remember how it feels to know someone, even a stranger, stopped what they were doing to pray for me and those I love in times of need or crisis.

In his book, Sacred Fire, Father Ron Rolheiser writes about facing our deaths in a way that encourages those we leave behind in faith and hope. He cites Jesus' passion, which most people interpret as his suffering and writes: "The English word passion takes its root in the latin passio, meaning "passivity"… Father Ron notes that Jesus is "…led away, manhandled by the authorities, whipped, helped in carrying his cross and ultimately nailed to that cross. After his arrest, like a patient in palliative care, he no longer does anything; others do it for him and to him."

So many of us fear the incapacities of old age, including me, including Burney. We want to die the moment immediately preceding the exit of our minds and mobility but it rarely goes that way. My father had what many would call a 'good death'. He lay down on his bed one morning fully clothed and died at the age of 80. He still lived independently and was able for the most part to care for himself but he had lost the bulk of his sight to macular degeneration. It is an especially cruel loss when we are deprived of the means to a skill at the heart of our identity. My father was an architect, an interior designer, a fashion plate, a devout reader and traveler. Everything about him was visual to the point where even after he had developed the big black dots in the center of his sight line, some of his long time clients continued to ask him to 'fluff' their houses claiming partial sight on him was better than full sight on anybody else. But once his eyes failed he fell into a morose silence that hardly ever lifted or allowed anyone access into his vulnerability. I have to say, I was relieved when he died but I don't look upon it as a particularly good death.

Father Ron suggests there is opportunity to share in the mystery of Jesus passion or passivity as we enter into our own passivity at the end of life: opportunity for others, particularly those we've cared for, to care for us and opportunity for us to receive. He writes: "Simply put, sometimes in our helplessness and passivity we can give something that is deeper than what we can give through our strength and activity." He cites James Hillman's: The Force Of Character and Lasting Life, saying: "When all the elderly are removed to retirement communities, the river flows smoothly back home. No disruptive rocks. Less character too."

Ah—character—the costly attribute. To accompany another in his or her diminishment requires that we diminish too. I think of my friend Laurel who took in her father in law near the end of his life. He viewed her as competition for her husband Dale's affection and she was rewarded for her care, cleaning and meals with subtle and not subtle comments and jabs through the days and years he lived with them. But when it came to the end, this man who had shown her so little regard told her those years had been the happiest of his life and thanked her.

Burney has begun to give away her death in small doses through her devotion to prayer and her desire to encourage younger women who view her as a mentor. She says she knows she's an old lady and mortality is probably near—though possibly not near enough as we have a family that features longevity. She's trying to set an example by embracing this stage of life—until an unpleasant encounter with the mirror starts her wondering all over again if she should order the plexi-derm she saw advertised on tv. At least, she says, she's not like the old lady she spotted the other day wearing a short ruffled dress designed for children and stockings bedazzled with decals—like a little old Alice in Wonderland. My father called these women 'creatures'—my mother is kinder and refers to them as 'poor dears'.

Burney endeavors to live faithfully to God, her children and grandchildren and her community daily but in that sense—she is still giving her life away. She would probably describe it as still being useful and I know she fears becoming senile and a burden. She says maybe she'll just stop talking one day and withdraw like her grandmother or my father. This I can't imagine (though I can see a few advantages) and I tell her: "Joe didn't stop talking." She says: "No, and he didn't stop asking questions either—like: Why did you all gang up on me and put me in an upholstered prison?"

My stepfathers last year brought out something beautiful in my mother though. She set aside the things of life she dearly loved, her home, her town, her activities and time. She set aside her ongoing complaints about her husband when he was active. She tolerated being forgotten as his wife, tolerated his questions and confusion every day, twice a day. She brought him to live near his children so that they could be part of his death too. And whereas he had often been prickly and difficult in his 'right' mind, he was approachable and soft in his dementia, giving his grandchildren access and affection.

I'm thinking about my friend Laurel again. Her husband Dale developed a sarcoma that was ultimately fatal. He did everything he knew to give away his death, to provide for her, to organize his affairs, to ease her, his children and grandchildren into the loss of a 44 year devoted marriage and family. She did everything she knew to accompany him, care for him and keep him

177

during the 4 years of his illness. There are many things that Laurel and Dale both did to give meaning to this brutal loss—but I like to tell of the day he finally went to hospice, shortly before he died.

The hospice was set to send an ambulance but Dale's sons canceled it. Adam, David, Michael and Mark, four of their six adult children, brought their father themselves and carried him tenderly through the door. Dale was, at that point, a passive actor in his death but that scene told much of the story of his life.

In that sense we spend our lives giving away our deaths. As my grandmother, Mama D began to shed her hearing and her appetite, eventually taking to her bed and surrendering the will to go on, I asked her if she had any thoughts about what she wanted in the way of a funeral. She whispered: "A great deal of sobbing". She got those sobs, decades later we are still mourning her, her love and delight in us, her humor and strength. In many ways she gave away her death by living well and living on in our memories. We love to quote her and tell stories—like the time she poured a drink on the head of my grandfathers fishing buddy for saying something sexist.

Burney is nearing 88. She's not as with it as she'd like but she is very much alive and with us. As the veil thins daily and thoughts of mortality and eternity become increasingly dominant, she talks to us about her will and estate. "How bout I pass out monopoly money and let everyone buy what they want." "No mom, no one wants to make a game out of it. Ask everyone what they want and if there's a conflict we'll work it out." And we will work it out. Because if there's one thing Burney has taught us it is that love is truly stronger than money or possessions, stronger than disagreements and in the end, just like Solomon said, stronger than death.

A GOOD SAMARITAN AND HER DRIVER

A few years ago I met my mother at the Nashville airport and, after a brief detour through a Wendy's drive-thru, we took the onramp for Interstate 40 east to Knoxville. We spent the drive chatting agreeably about nothing in particular: her flight, the green hills of Tennessee compared to the brown hills of California, news of my siblings and their families.

Somewhere between Crossville and Harriman as we descended the Cumberland Plateau, Burney mercifully stopped slurping her frosty long enough to say: "Did you see that boy?" "What boy?" "That boy walking on the shoulder of the interstate". "Mom, that was a man." "No, it was a boy and I think we should go back and get him." "Go back and get him?" "Yes, he might be picked up by a predator." "Mom, what if he's a predator? Kenny will kill me if we pick up a strange man walking along the interstate." "Well, I won't be able to sleep tonight if we don't go back."

At that point I knew that there was no use arguing and drove another five miles to the next exit. Hoping against hope that someone, a burly trucker, for instance, had taken pity on the stranger, I took my time turning around and heading back the way we had come. But before long my mother cried: "There! There he is."

We pulled onto the shoulder and he shuffled towards us. Burney got out of the car to 'vet' him. When she returned she said: "Well, you were right, he's not a boy but he needs our help." I asked her where he was going. "Georgia." "Georgia?" "Yes, Burney said, and I was thinking maybe we could find a bus station and drop him off."

Glancing around a particularly lonesome stretch of I-40 I told my mother I didn't think we'd have much luck locating a Greyhound depot in the near future. "Well, he'ssweet-and harmless I think, but he does smell pretty strongly of onions." "Oh boy..."

I was thinly stretched between equal parts guilt and reluctance. Unlike me, Burney routinely departs the grid to help someone in need who crosses her path or enters her sight line. She refers to this as her 'misplaced Messiah complex' though her compassion is real. The outcomes have been mixed but the disappointments never became deterrents. She returned home from her job at New York Life insurance in San Francisco once, telling us of a man she found sprawled on the sidewalk, leaning against a building moaning and calling out: "Help me, somebody please before the police come and take me away."

Burney said the man was well dressed in summer pinstripes so she ignored the reference to the police which might have alerted her to the man's history and assumed he was an upright citizen that had merely taken a fall. On further inspection, she discovered he was a drunk citizen and more or less dead weight. My mother looked around for help but no passer by offered a hand or even eye contact. Finally she stood in the sidewalk and physically blocked a man attempting to pass. Burney said the man looked stricken at her request for help, his frown expanding to a scowl when he glanced over at the slumped figure. They managed to hoist the drunk on his feet and he expressed his gratitude thanking my mother and Jesus—then peeing all over his pinstripes and the other man's elegant shoes.

Now, as I told the young man on the interstate to hop in the back seat of my Jeep, I wondered how this latest rescue attempt might play out, might end in pee.

Burney took over the introductions as if we had just arrived at a luncheon. His name was Chris and when I asked him what he wanted to do, he sat in the back seat, mute. I told him I wasn't going to Georgia but there was a large truck plaza about 30 miles up the road on the outskirts of Knoxville and I thought maybe he could find a hauler heading south willing to give him a lift. I waited for a reply. Nothing. Finally I took the next available exit, pulled over and faced him. He had bright blue eyes that might as well have been treated with the opaque privacy film of a bathroom window for all they revealed. Gazing at him I said, a bit more forcefully, "Chris, I need you to tell me how we can help you."

I suppose anyone gazing into my eyes at that moment would have had a fairly clear window to my frustration, fear and impatience. I longed to be free of him and to return to chatting about nothing with my mother.

Chris finally mumbled that the highway we had exited on, Highway 27 actually went to Georgia. I asked him if he wanted to get out where we had stopped but before he answered my mother piped up saying: "Let's just drive a little bit and see what we can find." What we found was a Dollar General, a couple of gas stations and a Cracker Barrel. I asked Chris if he had any money. "Two dollars and some change." Burney asked him if there was anyone he could call. He said, "Yeah but she ain't picking up." There's a reason for that. I thought.

I remembered a similar circumstance with a woman named Lucy, a new-comer to Burney's AA meeting who needed a place to stay after her own mother had washed her hands of her. My mother, once again seduced by the fact that Lucy was well groomed and attractively dressed, offered Lucy her newly redecorated guest quarters.

Initially all went well, Lucy got a job and a car from her mother who, impressed by Burney's generosity, decided to pitch in too. Burney crowed to me and my siblings: "You see, all Lucy needed was someone to take a chance on her!"

Things went well for a time until Lucy gradually stopped showing up for meals and eventually stopped materializing at all. Burney made a few attempts to check on her, crossing the covered patio that separated the guest room from the main house and calling through the door to ask if she was all right. Lucy said she'd been sick but otherwise was fine and not to worry.

Fortunately my sister Windsor arrived for a visit and when she heard about Lucy who was now all but invisible, she asked our mother when she had last actually seen the woman. Burney couldn't recall and said she hadn't wanted to disturb her since she wasn't feeling well. Then she wondered aloud if maybe Lucy was drinking. Windsor said there was one way to find out and marched across the breezeway.

Before isolating herself, Lucy had visited several food banks and thrift stores. The room was overflowing with vast quantities of nonperishables like cases of cup o soup, oatmeal, microwave popcorn and a microwave. Clothing was stacked everywhere but the closet—and the bathroom sink, an unwilling repository for food waste was backed up and unusable. Then there was the carpet. Lucy apparently preferred red wine and it looked as though at least a glass or two from each jug had hit the floor.

My mother called me later and said Windsor's usual supply of the 'milk of human kindness' had instantly dried up and she demanded that Lucy pack her bags. She escorted Lucy off the property herself to see that there were no shenanigans and warned her off any thoughts of returning. But even as Windsor helped our mother in the arduous process of restoring order to the guest room, she knew, as did I, the next freeloader was on the way—probably neatly dressed and needing someone to take a chance on them.

I glanced at Chris again, he was neither neatly nor shabbily dressed and he didn't seem to want much of anything from us. We made a few more suggestions, all of which were met with silence. But eventually he said: "You can let me out here." I pulled into a Cracker Barrel parking lot and gave him $20.00. Later I found his two dollars and change wadded up in the back seat. My mother told him we'd be praying for him to get safely back to Georgia and I wondered when he had last heard any words of concern.

As I expected, everyone we mentioned the incident to told us we were insane to pick him up. Our friend in Knoxville, Teenie, later served us dinner and a lecture. She relented a bit though and said: "Well, you two are good Samaritans". I quickly corrected her and said, "No, one of us is a good Samaritan and the other one is merely easily manipulated".

Currently Burney has down-sized to a two bedroom house and boasted to me recently that she has confined overnight visitors to family members. "That's because you only have one bathroom mom—and even that wouldn't stop you."

I was serious—but only half serious—because I appreciate my mothers extended hand, stretched out in full, to help, to comfort, to welcome, to share her goods. Some people would dismiss her as another white savior of means attempting to absolve her guilt—and there is certainly some of that. But I think Burney would say she is responding to Jesus' words to freely give as we have freely been given. Even then, sometimes in our more heated political exchanges she tells me with Republican assurance that a free hand is a hand that is bitten repeatedly as she argues for fewer government interventions and provisions.

I struggle too—to know when to reach out and when to stand back, when to open my home, my heart, my wallet and certainly my car door to people in need. Most of the time when I look the other way it's because I don't want to clean up the mess or lose something I care about. But I know about possibility and that any person at any time can step into a better way of living no matter how many opportunities they've blown. I know too that many of us need a free hand here and there no matter where we come from or how we got where we are. I think of all the people who were weary of my repeated disasters—like Burney, all the people who paid dearly for their proximity to me—like Burney. What we can offer to another person, in addition to sharing our goods, is our hope for them.

So I hope Chris made it back to Georgia in one piece, I hope my mother's prayers are answered and that he finds his solid ground. Maybe all he needed was for someone to take a chance on him

FAITH

The everything in a word, the music written on our souls, pray out loud, pray in silence, pray in deed, carry it forward.

INSTEAD, HE RESTORED MY SOUL

My introduction to poetry was the book of Psalms, written in the King James:

The Lord is my shepherd, I shall not want
He maketh me to lie down in green pastures,
He leadeth me beside still waters
He restoreth my soul

My maternal grandmother, Neel, was a school teacher and ran a strict household. Burney said Neel favored switches for a time as a punishment. I laughed and told her: "I had a few unpleasant run-ins with switches too—with you. In fact, as I recall, you sent me out a few times to cut my own." She conveniently does not remember this.

Eventually my grandmother replaced the switches with two types of discipline: memorizing scripture and shelling the pecans that arrived by the barrel full from my great grandfather's plantation in South Carolina. These methods differed wildly. Pecan shells have sharp edges that nick tender hands and release a tannin that stains and can only be removed with lava soap. Burney said the pads of her fingers will never be the same—she still has scars.

187

The tedium of scripture memorization is in the rote, over and over, trying to keep the 'thees and thous' straight. For misbehaving children it hardly feels like green pastures and still waters—more like an endless procession of words that either begin or end with 'th'. Somewhere in the monotony though a word or a phrase might catch and take hold, returning again and again, not to tear or scar but to mend and heal.

He leadeth me in the paths of righteousness
for His name's sake
Yea, though I walk through the valley
of the shadow of death, I will fear no evil
for Thou art with me
Thy rod and thy staff they comfort me

Burney went on to memorize many passages of scripture throughout both the old and new testaments. She was further encouraged by her Sunday school teacher, Mrs. Henigar who wisely understood the irresistible pull of shiny things and awarded gold stars on a big chart for mastering the weekly verse. My mother, never one to shrink from competition, knew she had the edge of a long line of preparation and handily filled the chart spaces next to her name with stars. I don't know that the promises contained in the verses penetrated her soul—then. Because even as a child she found herself in the shadow of death with the loss of her baby brother and initially I think she experienced more confusion than comfort. There is always the lingering question—if God is good and if I am good—why do I have to walk through the valley of the shadow of death at all? But if we have courage for the question, it can be the gateway to a lifelong conversation that is sometimes a song, sometimes a lament, sometimes a long period of silence but rarely empty. For me, that conversation began with a bible.

Christians refer to scripture as 'The Word'. The gospel of John begins with a declaration of Jesus as Gods Word to the world and the radiant source of life and light:

188

In the beginning was the Word
And the Word was with God
And the Word was God

Declaring that the word of God is 'alive and powerful' the book of Hebrews goes on to say:

By faith we understand that the worlds were framed by the word of God,
so that the things which are seen
were not made by the things which are visible.

Thus in response to the question, what's in a word? In the realm of the Spirit, it would not be a stretch to answer: everything.

Burney didn't dole out bible memory as a punishment though she did favor a few threat verses to repeat to me when I was behaving badly. And for a long stretch, pretty much all the time, I was behaving badly. I heard about the millstones, I heard about how nothing ("nothing, Ashley") is hidden from God, I heard it and frankly, I did tremble. I encountered the scripture more as evidence of a fierce rod of reproof than a loving shepherd's staff.

I know my mother was trying anything and everything to put the brakes on a runaway locomotive of self-will. I know she thought that if I wasn't paying the slightest attention to her admonitions, maybe I could be swayed by a higher authority. But I had an addicts destiny to play out and I did. When I had exhausted every bit of promise that drugs and alcohol offered me and was buried alive in the wreckage of it all, I became slightly teachable, slightly open to the idea that maybe there was another way. I understood from Sunday school that God was a God of justice. What I didn't know, what I still have trouble comprehending is that the justice of God is mercy. I anticipated He might destroy me. Instead, He restored my soul.

Before teaching a course on Philippians at a church I attended, one of the facilitators had an introductory 'debriefing session' for those people in her group whose experiences of bible study in the hands of their teachers and preachers—and even their parents—were far more punishing than switches

189

and pecan shells. For many the Good News is often anything but, and people use the scripture to justify and amplify their own beliefs—and pathologies. I know too that when it comes to interpreting the mind of God—who framed the worlds with a word—all of us will get it wrong somewhere.

But in the midst of all the arguing and parsing over interpretation, I only know this, nearly every day I open the word and find life. It is where I meet Jesus and am struck all over again by the graciousness that flows from his mouth. I find story after story from Genesis through the Revelation of flawed, failed human beings reignited with purpose and even new and clearly farfetched names by the maker of the universe who calls what is out of what is not. It is where the prophets document history, driven by people full of hubris and self will, repeating again and again—and right along with it, mercy and restoration. I see others like myself in much of it—but more importantly, pulsing at the heart, I see the one who knows me well and loves me still. Because it was love that changed me and continues to change me. And it is the desire to embody that love that drives me on.

Thou preparest a table for me in the presence of mine enemies
Thou anointest my head with oil
My cup overfloweth
Surely goodness and mercy shall follow me all the days of my life
And I shall dwell in the house of The Lord forever

Burney says one of the many indignities of old age is interrupted sleep. And as more than a few of us know from Lady Melisandre in A Song Of Fire and Ice, if not personal experience, "The night is dark and full of terrors." When my mother wakes to her heart pounding with apprehension and concerns—for her children and grandchildren, for the world that is now foreign and fearful to her, for her health and that of others, she begins to recite the verses of peace and refuge she learned as a child.

So often we encounter our worst enemies in the ghetto of our own minds. I continue to memorize scripture as an antidote not only for worry but for self absorbed, obsessive thoughts and find a table full of promise, a cup that

190

spills hope and comfort along with course correction and an ever increasing desire to be transformed and renewed. Burney meditates on her favorite passages in the dark and that same hope that anchors her soul fills her heart and quiets the panic until at last she sleeps, dreaming perhaps of the house that lies beyond imagination where one day she will continue her conversation face to face.

Of all the gifts my mother has laid before me again and again, even when I refused saying I didn't like the wrapping and I didn't want what was essentially hers, faith and a love of the scriptures, once received as my own, have become the bedrock of my life. This is not to say that Burney and I think and interpret alike—we don't. But that's the beauty of it, God meets us and reveals himself to us as we are, he does not urge us to rally round the dogma or join together in lockstep—though some do. Instead he offers to set us free and restore our souls.

A TREASURY OF HYMNS

In our household regular church attendance was a given. No excuse, short of measurable illness, was an acceptable pass on any Sunday. Once, I managed to get my hands on some turquoise eye shadow somewhere (chances are good I stole it) and had coated my eyelids quite seductively, I felt. My stepfather caught the glare of it in his rearview mirror and found plenty of time to return home, have me remove it and get us to church on time. We were maddeningly early arrivals—every week.

I considered this 'family rule' harassment and was determined to make someone, my mother, pay. I squirmed and slumped in the pew, casting about for some form of entertainment to fill the long Presbyterian hour before me. I know now I should have been grateful. If we were Episcopalian, it would have been an hour and a half, Church of Christ would have neared the two hour mark and Pentecostals—I shudder to think.

We sat in the same pew, second on the right, every week and my entertainment options were slim. I played with the registration pad until my mother took it away from me and then, reluctant to pick up a bible and read—which might please her, I took up the hymnal, cracking it open and scanning song after song hoping to distract her by telegraphing my inattention to the pulpit. I should have caught on to the fact that never once did she take the hymnal out of my hands. In fact, rather than disturbing her worship, she paid me no mind at all. I was free to roam page after page of the sacred songs we sing to affirm our faith.

My husband Kenny likes to say his experience of a deepening faith has been subtle, like grass growing. So too my attachment to hymns—I knew I had my favorites to sing but I didn't know they were writing themselves on my soul in the midst of my rebellion. I didn't notice the tiny flutter of my heart when the organist would play the anthemic opening to Holy Holy Holy or Love Divine All Loves Excelling. Once I saw my father tear up on Easter Sunday as he sang Christ The Lord Is Risen Today in his gravel-paved monotone. I was not privy to his inner life and pain then but I did feel the hope of redemption in the melody and I cried a little too. My attention in those days was fully tuned to top forty radio and popular music. The only gospel music I claimed was black gospel. I wore out an album called "Let Us Go Into The House Of The Lord" by the Edwin Hawkins singers that featured a hit called "O Happy Day" sung by Dorothy Morrison. It was recorded in a sanctuary, the sound and the soloists are muffled and uneven, but it's a great example of the truth that music, music from the soul, transcends all limitations.

Years later, when my church attendance was sketchy at best, when I had started the descent into alcoholism and drug addiction and was beginning to comprehend true despair, these Sunday morning songs returned to me unbidden. There's a place of wakefulness among addicts, often just before dawn where we are too high too sleep and too low to function. I used to sit in a rocking chair in my living room feeling the dread, hating the birds, waiting for my eyes to close for a little while. In those in between unfocused stretches, bits of hymn refrains would drop into my conscious mind, teardrop shaped and gentle. They felt like love notes from a God I hardly knew. They gave me the idea that maybe I could live.

Jesus sought me when a stranger
Wandering from the fold of God
He to rescue me from danger
Bought me with His precious blood

I suppose my faith was like the grass too because I could feel the light in those moments of darkness—though I was not yet ready to accept its warmth.

Once I came into the 'fold of God' and received a storehouse of gifts, including a path to sobriety, I returned to the hymns often, voluntarily, creating my own arrangements and playing them in concert. I was equally drawn to Black Gospel. On the surface the two styles are vastly different. Hymns are often high church with complex melodies and lofty language, though the music is just as likely to have evolved from a 16th century drinking song as from Mozart. Black Gospel is a prime example of early American roots music, with simple, direct, colloquial lyrics and music that tends to the rhythm and blues side.

The similarity that strikes me is that so many of these songs of devotion were born of suffering. Hundreds of hymns were written by people with profound illnesses, disabilities and crushing loss. The Gospel songs were written, often in the fields, by African Americans forced into brutal slavery who brought a habit of singing their way through the events of the day from the dark continent that was their home. And yet, along with the mourning strains, there is solace, hope and great joy in both of these styles of music.

Jesus, the man of sorrows, said clearly we would experience suffering in this world, though that message can be lost in the appeal of a victorious religious road to prosperity and success.

But belonging to Christ offers us the opportunity to discover that the gifts employed in the worst hard times, in unbearable crucibles often become sources of strength, faith and pearls of great price to give to others. I love to think of how the writers of hymns and gospel songs alike were creating in response to their own experience of the presence of The Lord. They did it because they could, they did it to survive, to speak what they believed into an impoverished void, to express their longings and hope. They didn't know their music would sooth and lift the hearts of literally millions of people for centuries. They did not know their suffering would matter.

But so it is—a well used talent can and should exceed and outlive us. I am keenly attached to my own songs as an expression of my identity and I write with the hope that any of my compositions will take on a life of its own and have value to others. But for me, the hymns and spirituals occupy consecrated real estate and shine like the precious metal that waits in the furnace until the smith can see his image. They pierce my soul in a singular way that leads me to God and is utterly restorative. They are welcome companions as I walk through a world teeming with life and loss.

My mother learned many of the hymns from her mother and grandmother. That's another aspect of hymnody that is precious to me. I'm a devout rock and roll lover and many of my favorite albums would have been dismissed as 'banging and clanging' by my grandmother—and my great grandmother would have covered her ears and merely looked puzzled. We can agree, however, on sacred music and that mutual love links the generations, like the communion of saints.

When Burney returned to live in Sonoma County, she gave up a traditional protestant worship service to attend a non denominational church where my brother, Paul was one of the pastors. She loves the church, loves the preaching, loves the people, hates the music. When I called to ask her which hymns were her favorites, she would interrupt her own reminiscence with complaints: "Well, as I get older, I particularly love Abide With Me. Honestly I get so put out with these modern worship bands. Can't they take off their hats and tuck in their shirts? It's irreverent!" "It's their style mom. What else?" "Do you know He Giveth More Grace? I can't sing that one without weeping."

Then she's off on another tirade about a church she recently visited: "Honestly, there's something so unpleasant about someone leading music with his stomach hanging over his pants. It's just not conducive to worship." She rails on for a few more minutes and then, her critical commentary exhausted for the moment, she sings a few lines of Annie Flint Johnson's hymn, He Giveth More Grace in her now fluttery soprano:

His love has no limits, His grace has no measure,
His power no boundary known unto men

196

For out of His infinite riches in Jesus
He giveth, and giveth, and giveth again.

The world and the church are full of all types of worship music now. Personally I have less trouble with an untucked shirt or stomach than with the recycled chord structures and language that dominate modern worship. But I know while I stand there judging, someone else is filled with praise and weeping. I know too when my mother and I are on opposite sides of an issue and cannot agree, we can sing together. My friend Amy said when her parents had fallen into dementia and were unable to have even the simplest conversations, she brought a guitar to the nursing home and they found their voices in the sacred songs they'd sung all their lives. The songs became the conversation.

There is music that is written on our souls, often from our earliest experience of God and faith. For Burney it is hymns, for me it is hymns and traditional gospel, for my husband Kenny it's the songs sung in Hebrew by the ancient cantor in his synagogue in Cleveland. All of it is designed to take us out of ourselves and put the focus on a creator who is generous and unstinting, who provides a means and a melody for anybody that wants it. Annie had it right—while we are down here arguing about the merits and mediocrity of worship music to 'give to God', God himself is giving and giving and giving again—to us.

TONGUES OF MEN AND ANGELS

Over the last few years, I've felt an increasing desire to petition less and listen more in prayer. I have no patriarchal issues when it comes to 'God the Father'—probably because of the unmet longings left behind in my relationship with my own father. I love to imagine myself resting in the hands, the strong tender hands that hold the world. But even resting, I'm usually chirping. Just as my children come to their father with requests for counsel, for insurance, for his reservoir of experience, for his wallet, I usually have a request list of my own when I pray: How do I do this? Can I have that? Can you do such and such for so and so? Jesus, as usual, was different. His food, he said, his want, his will was the will of the Father. He had his own heartfelt petitions but always leavened with "nevertheless, not my will but Thine..." So—with varying degrees of success I endeavor to stop talking and turn to contemplation.

I've never been particularly good at meditation. Even in silence, the beehive in my head is buzzing away. Increasingly though, that is changing. I have an inexplicable desire to empty my mind and fill it with knowledge of Jesus, unexpected and surprising. Who is this man? I want to know and the more I sit, the more I want to sit. I was astonished one day to find that I had been in the chair for 30 minutes reflecting. In all honesty, there were more than a few moments of considering the plans for the day ahead and thinking about various situations but when I became aware my mind had wandered, I returned to the verse I'd read that day, listened to birds—the faithful retinue of the sun and set my thoughts again on the Lord. I don't hear him speak directly to me often—most of what I get is proximity, the nearness that fills the room with peace.

And I don't think I will ever return to my old style of prayer, though I have no problem confiding my deepest longings and petitions. The difference now is I tell him and leave it there. I'm far more interested in his presence than any circumstance—maybe because I'm in my sixties and that much closer to 'face to face' but I can't think of a better or sweeter use of my time.

Martin Luther wrote: "A good prayer mustn't be too long. Do not draw it out. Prayer ought to be frequent and fervent." I would especially apply this maxim to corporate prayer. I have personally never been big on public petition and find lengthy group intercession tedious. There are many prayers that I love and say often: the Lord's Prayer, the Serenity Prayer (including the profane shortcut version), the 3rd and 7th step prayers from the AA Big Book, Thomas Merton's Prayer That Anyone Can Pray, the Prayer of St Francis, the Prayer of St. Patrick. All of these are prayers I know by heart and love to repeat. They are not only eloquent and poetic, they have a beginning and an end. Sitting in a room full of people warming up to the sounds of their own voices and going on and on and on, well clearly it brings out the worst in me. I know this intolerance is a character defect, I know that prayer vigils are deeply meaningful to people and that the problem is mine. I've been an offense to friends who enjoy praying out loud when before they commence I caution them to 'keep it brief please'. I want to interrupt people fervently requesting not only their desires but also outlining every detail of the method and the means. I want to demand that the group chant one round of "Thy will be done" and then actually be done. Truthfully, I don't even pretend to like it—with one exception, my mother.

When Burney prays it's as if she has been anointed for that moment. She speaks from her heart but her choice of words combined with bits of verse from her storehouse of scripture memory make each prayer like a hymn.

Before my nephew Zach's wedding to his wife Abbie, my mother added her prayers at a breakfast one morning declaring "What a precious bride for our beloved Zach! Father I pray for the day and not just for the day but for the rest of their lives together that Jesus will be the center and rock upon which they build their house. Help them to remember when the hard times come, as they inevitably do, that these too pass and you will never leave them or forsake them."

Every morning begins with a gratitude list in which Burney thanks God for whatever is on her heart: "...life itself, a loving family who enjoy one another for the most part, the blessings of comfort, lovely homes to live in, cars to drive, gas in the tank, all things we take for granted until they are absent. Thank you for filling our hearts with the desire to know you and belong to you because if you didn't give it, we wouldn't have it." She prays for wise counsel for those in power and against the abuses of that power. She asks God to keep watch over the door of her mouth that she might choose her words carefully and for the discernment of the holy spirit that she would focus not on the negative but on the sovereign Lord.

Burney has always had a rich vocabulary and I know that's part of the appeal for me but I ask her about the foundations of her prayer life. She says she never wanted to present God with a 'letter to Santa Claus list'; she prays the scriptures instead, returning his own words back to him as she prays "because if it's not what he wants, I don't want it either." I know what she means—though I can't say I always agree. There's plenty of stuff I want that God doesn't seem to want for me. But in the long game—and life in Christ is always the long game—I sometimes see the larger picture unfold and I realize what initially felt petty and withholding, was the ultimate wisdom in its fullness.

Burney says she began by praying the Psalms and returns often to favorite verses. My own scripture memorization is prompted by a desire for something and someone in my head other than me and because my mother's prayers are steeped in the truth from the page, not only do I sit still for them, I relish them and consider them gifts for the day. I know too that when Burney could not hold her tongue with me, when every word felt like an indictment, some part of her knew that no threat had the power to save me, no criticism had the power to fix me and the anger that poured from her mouth was shaped by fear that I wouldn't live long enough to live. But she was not without a prayer.

My mother prayed faithfully for me—often on her knees. She asked God to save me, to restore me, to bring a spouse that I could build a family and a life with, to give me purpose and a place for my gifts in this world. And he did. Burney has continued to pray for my daughter, Becca, her first grand-daughter. She has prayed in hospitals when Becca's heroin use led to staph infections, she prays in the halfway houses, she prays through the long absences. Both of us understand that answered prayer does not necessarily include what we want. Both of us believe there will be an answer though—for Becca's good and our good too.

In contemplative prayer, Thomas Keating teaches us to move beyond words, to experience the presence of God as "....closer than breathing, closer than thinking, closer than consciousness itself." Often it is only when my own words are spent and I sit in silence that I begin to sense the nearness and weight of the love of Jesus who is the anchor of my soul.

So it is—we pray out loud, we pray in silence, we pray in deed. We pray with the hope that eventually our lives will become a prayer. Maybe that's why my great grandmother stopped talking at the end of her life, maybe she'd said all she had to say and was listening to Gods prayer for her as she prepared to meet him. Maybe the veil split as she neared the end and she knew as Julian of Norwich knew: "All shall be well and all shall be well and all manner of things shall be well." Amen.

PASS THE PEACE

Burney returned to Knoxville for a visit a year ago. Her trips home (would she still call it home?) are infrequent now as the journey becomes increasingly old lady arduous. We arrange for a wheel chair to provide taxi service to and from the gates and I find her at baggage anxiously examining the contents on the belt. She skips her usual warm greeting and says: "I don't see my bag, I bought a pink suitcase thinking mine would be the only one but just look!" I count three and tell her not to worry, the belt is still running and the bags are still loading. I ask if any of the three are hers, "No—pink! One of those is more lavender and the other looks red." That's how it is with Burney. Sometimes you lean in for a hug and get a lesson in the color wheel instead.

Delinquent bag eventually in hand we take the well worn interstate 40 from Nashville to Knoxville. Nearly every social hour is spoken for on this trip but Sunday morning there will be no lingering over coffee with our friend Teenie. When the church bells ring my mother wants to be in the sanctuary. She will settle for the Presbyterian church in Sequoyah Hills but prefers First Presbyterian downtown where her family attended. Burney wants to relive her childhood sabbaths on the fifth row pew. She wants to sit in the light filled sanctuary, gaze at the splendid mosaic of Jesus above the altar with his arms outstretched surrounded by the stained glass windows she knows by heart. My mother has endured modern worship songs, baggy jeans and untucked shirts, not silently, not stoically or cheerfully—but consistently and she is ready, more than ready, for a choir in robes and a well played pipe organ.

Burney lifts each uncluttered memory from its treasure box: the ladies in their hats, particularly Mrs Patterson who wore one adorned with egret feathers that fanned over her perfectly white hair, creating a halo and the men in their sharp suits and polished shoes dressed like they were coming to meet the king, which of course, they were. She's even savoring the unpleasant moments when a skirmish with one of her sisters would result in her mother's large hand quietly enclosing her own to deliver a little pressure and a little pain until tranquility was restored.

It's raining when we set out for the early service. My sister Windsor, also in town for the visit says she'll meet us there and save us a seat. But we arrive to find her standing on the sidewalk out front declaring the church empty. I don't really care one way or the other, though I would like to visit the cemetery on the property and commune with the saints that include numerous luminaries like James White, the founder of Knoxville and William Blount, governor of the Southwest territory that eventually became Tennessee. I love old cemeteries. I have threatened to haunt my family if they reduce me to cremains and put me in a pasture with a flat marker for easier mowing and a plastic bouquet. I want a plain pine box, a tree and a headstone—though in response to my insistence my epitaph may well read—"Demanding to the end"

I have hardly finished parallel parking when Windsor returns to announce she has found the chapel—and the people.

The chapel is a peaceful, pleasant space but lacks the grandeur of the sanctuary. We'll call that: 'let down number one.' On this morning the senior pastor has given the pulpit to a recent seminary graduate who begins with an illustration of the body of Christ as either 'turnip people' or 'collard green people'. It must have been intended as a sly reference to the fact that the church was built on a turnip patch in 1792 but for Burney it's 'let down number two': "What kind of message is this? she says. I came for a sermon but all he talked about was vegetables"

Let down number three was the absence of any mention of Jesus in the lesson. For me there was a let down number four when the newly minted preacher quoted the poet Rainier Maria Rilke, mispronouncing his name as Wilke and referring to him as a 'she'.

After the sermon we take a page out of Anglican liturgy and pass the peace. The typical greeting is to shake hands and bid those around us the 'peace of Christ'. Burney takes it a step further and says in a firm voice to her neighbors: "The peace of the Lord Jesus be with you." I can tell by her delivery that she has an agenda and I ask her later: "Mom did you pass the peace of the Lord Jesus intentionally?" "Yes, she says. I feel like people rush through it like they're embarrassed; sometimes they don't mention Jesus at all, they say: 'Peace be with you'. They might as well be saying: 'May the force be with you' if they're not going to give credit where credit is due. Personally, I need the peace of The Lord Jesus and I bet they do too so I spell it out."

She doesn't leave that personal peace on the pew with her bulletin when she exits the chapel either. Every day she turns her life and her will over to the care of Christ and invites Him into every aspect of her life—even her car. People like to joke about the ridiculousness of asking God, the King of the universe to supply them with a parking space. Maybe so but I wonder how much road rage can be traced to driving in interminable circles trying to find a place to land.

Burney does not view Jesus as her co-pilot, she sees Him as her shield against idiot drivers and other agents of evil. She prays for maximum protection and a legion of angels forming a winged barrier around her car. She says: "Of course, I'll do my part and drive responsibly." To which I think: 'more or less, lately less.'

But my mother does not subscribe to any kind of prosperity gospel, she takes the world as is, and if the wheels come off and she encounters her demise suddenly on some highway of life, she knows she has a ready escort to meet her maker in the air.

These seeds of reliance on the peace and provision of the Lord Jesus were sown in this church. First by the pastor Dr. McGukin who came repeatedly to visit my grandparents Neel and Paul and to invite them to church, though Neel, unmoved by his Scottish brogue, never asked him in or came to church herself, going only so far as to send Paul to drop the children off for Sunday school. Then Burney's little brother and Paul and Neel's only son Michael died and my grandmother was swept into the kind of grief that often requires something not in this world to survive. She turned to the pastor she had scorned and his God for rescue.

My mother found another wellspring of living water in her Sunday School class with a woman named Emily Heniger who was plain and even homely by any physical standards but was so lit from within, Burney found her irresistible and remembers visiting her at her home, sitting on her porch and shelling beans from the garden, anything to be in her presence.

Mrs. Heniger lost her husband prematurely to cancer and while he was hospitalized one of their sons was killed in a car accident. My mother asked her how in the world she could go on believing in the face of such senseless unspeakable loss. Mrs. Heniger looked at her with great kindness and compassion and said: "Burney, the joy of The Lord is my strength" That was my mothers first notion of the possibility that the joy of God was irrelevant to circumstance.

Memory is a funny thing. Often the memories I most cherish have been smoothed and polished to some sort of perfection over the years that never existed in the first place. But there are a few that have so shaped or redirected me that I am very clear about the accuracy of them. I think Burney's experience of First Presbyterian resides in her soul with that kind of crystallized recollection. She sighs on the return drive to Teenie's house and says: "Well, I guess you can't go back" "No, you can't." I say.

"But you can carry it forward."

IF NOT HAPPILY EVER AFTER

The poet, Czeslaw Milosz wrote: "When a writer is born into a family, the family is finished." You could look at the last word from two angles: finished as complete or finished as lost. I think about the days when my first thought in relation to my mother was 'How can I get away from this woman?' and feel the latter but these days it's the former I gratefully inhabit.

In hearing and sharing these stories I'm reminded of t s eliot's description of the still point in his poem burnt norton:

"at the still point of the turning world
neither flesh nor fleshless
neither from nor towards
at the still point, there the dance is
but neither arrest nor movement and do not call it fixity
where past and future are gathered. neither movement from nor towards
neither descent or decline. except for the point, the still point
there would be no dance, and there is only the dance."

As I carry on with the dance of my own life, I feel my mother's presence, and not only hers but that of my entire family, not as the rock that will sink me but as a weight that grounds me. It's all there where past and future gather—the beautiful and rotten, the whole and broken.

I know not all of us find real peace or any peace for that matter with our mothers but my experience and my hope is that a broader lens and perspective will blunt the pointy end and give understanding and even compassion for our parents, for ourselves and for the ongoing dance we are born into. Because like it or not, the dance remains at our core and will inform our lives from beginning to end.

We might as well dosey doe.

Ashley Cleveland and Burney Sheeks

ASHLEY CLEVELAND

Ashley Cleveland is a three time Grammy award winning singer songwriter. She is an author, speaker and the subject of an award winning feature length documentary, "Who's The Girl." Ashley's first book, a memoir, "Little Black Sheep" was released in 2013 by D.C. Cook publishing. She has a certificate in spiritual direction and is a pastoral associate at Church of the Redeemer in Nashville. She lives with her husband in Franklin, Tennessee and has three adult children.

Also by Ashley Cleveland:
LITTLE BLACK SHEEP

Cover Design by The Visual Strategist
Cover page photo of Burney by Carissa Graham
Photo of Ashley and Burney by Jennie Haug

CPSIA information can be obtained
at www.ICGtesting.com
Printed in the USA
LVHW030936130222
710985LV00019B/1342